COUNSELING PEOPLE WHO HAVE KILLED OTHER PEOPLE

DR. RICHARD K. NONGARD
& DAVID PARKE

NOTE REGARDING ONLINE PIRACY

As the original purchaser of this online document you are entitled to enjoy the material contained within. You have also done the right thing my making an investment in your success. Please DO NOT SHARE this online with others who have not paid for it.

The therapy industry is a large industry, and many therapists are no longer releasing online books or videos because online piracy steals the work of the original creator. Piracy keeps writers and experts from being willing to share. Everyone must earn a living, and original products are the lifeblood of continued learning in the therapy industry.

It is illegal to share this file. It is protected under international copyright law. Violators of copyright face stiff fines and risk jail in some cases.

We will prosecute any copyright infringement.

Do not copy, e-mail to others, post online, or distribute copies in any way.

COUNSELING PEOPLE WHO HAVE KILLED OTHER PEOPLE

By Dr. Richard K. Nongard and David Parke

ISBN-13: 978-1720557746 | ISBN-10: 1720557748

Printed in the United States of America

by PeachTree Professional Education, Inc.

Peachtree Professional Education, Inc.
Scottsdale, Arizona
(918) 236-6116

www.FastCEUs.com

www.RichardNongard.com

KEYNOTE SPEAKING, CONFERENCE TRAINING, AND IN-HOUSE TRAINING FOR PROFESSIONAL GROUPS

Dr. Richard K. Nongard and David Parke, are available together or separately to provide valuable training on this subject or other topics related to leadership, counseling and helping other people.

Bring Dr. Richard K. Nongard and/or David Parke to your professional group.

Contact Information:

Dr. Richard K. Nongard

Peachtree Professional Education, Inc.

15560 N. Frank L. Wright Blvd. B4-118 Scottsdale, AZ 85260

(918) 236-6116 or (702) 488-9640

richard@fastceus.com or visit www.RichardNongard.com

ABOUT THE AUTHORS

Dr. Richard K. Nongard

The executive director of Peachtree Professional Education and president of the International Certifying Board of Clinical Hypnotherapy, Nongard holds degrees in both counseling and ministry. He has a doctorate in Transformational Leadership (Cultural Transformation) form Bakke Graduate University and a Master's Degree in Counseling from Liberty University. Before entering private practice as a licensed marriage and family therapist and certified clinical hypnotherapist, he worked as a minister in several churches.

Nongard's work with substance abusers led him to work with clients suffering from PTSD, some of whom had killed other human beings due malevolence, accident, or self-defense. His background in ministry and therapy, combined with the experience of working with this unique population, provided him with the tools to affect his clients in a very positive way.

David Parke

Before becoming a board-certified coach through the Center for Credentialing and Education who specializes in strategic intervention, hypnosis, and neurolinguistic programming, David Parke spent most of his adult life in the military, serving as a Navy diver and an Army Ranger. He spent eight years as a military advisor in Iraq and Afghanistan. Because of his background, he has first-hand experience with populations who have taken lives and may experience PTSD.

TABLE OF CONTENTS

Introduction

YOUR MISSION

This book grew out of a series of workshops that we did. As we presented this material at several different locations, it was really interesting to hear the unique cases that therapists were dealing with. One lady came because she had worked with a young female who, in a situation of self-protection, had taken a perpetrator's life. Others worked with an emphasis on military personnel. The models for how people respond and the needs they display are uniquely different.

In this book, we're going to provide you with a number of different resource tools so that you'll actually be able to utilize the strategies with the clients that are on your caseload.

The objectives are pretty simple. These are the broad things we will address:

Identify the praxeological needs of clients who have killed

When we use the word praxeological, people often say, "I'm not sure I've heard of praxes. Is that a real word?" It's actually a great word, because it means all-encompassing. It's not just the psychological needs, like a therapist might be accustomed to addressing. It's not just the spiritual needs, like a minister might be accustomed to addressing. It's not just a social or organizational set of needs, like a soldier or a military unit might deal with.

Praxeology is looking at a person from a perspective of their entire being and their entire experiences. We're going to look at the unique needs of those who have killed other people and look at those needs from a number of different perspectives.

Develop strategies for supporting those who have taken a life, especially in the line of duty

A lot of times, one of the very first things that happens if somebody has killed in the line of duty is they're immediately removed from their environment, from their support systems—in a sense, from their family—in order to assess their needs.

But in removing them from that environment, they are separated from a lot of the resources that they naturally have—their support mechanisms.

For example, a city bus driver accidentally killed a pedestrian who was crossing the street. The pedestrian was jaywalking, and the city employee driving the bus unintentionally and unfortunately killed that person.

The driver had worked for the city for twenty-eight years as a bus driver. His job was how he derived his identity. His coworkers were his family. But the mandatory investigative period removed him from those people who were most likely to support him, and in the isolation over a two-week inquiry period—required primarily to satisfy the needs of politicians—he became very depressed, in fact, suicidal. He became a person who was himself at risk through no fault of his own.

We see this with law enforcement, military, and many other settings.

In the military, it's a little bit different because there's the expectation that a soldier probably will kill. What happens after any incident, though, for the regular military (not for the special operations forces) is an immediate investigation to determine whether or not the shooting was justified. The same holds true for police officers.

Almost immediately, there's an accusatory phase in which the soldier or officer is asked, "Did you do wrong here?" A person may have their own ideas or own questions on their mind. As a therapist, you know that there is probably a state of confusion that happens, and the person is more susceptible to suggestion when they're confused.

If they're automatically besieged by accusations, then they may take that on board as "I did something wrong" when perhaps they didn't feel that way to begin with.

It's interesting to see how suggestions—and those are really almost hypnotic suggestions—are given to folks unintentionally through the processes. This occurs in a variety of different contexts.

Examine methods to stabilize the family and personal systems of those who have killed

In most cases, attention is on the person who has taken the life of another person, whether that is through malevolence, by accident, in the line of duty, or in any other circumstance or situation.

The family is that stabilizing force in our client's life, and often our processes don't provide the support necessarily to those families for those who are dealing with this issue. It becomes the metaphorical elephant in the living room that nobody ever talks about. It's there, and the whole family can see it, but nobody ever mentions it.

There's an old saying in addiction counseling: "You're only as sick as your secrets." The need to bring family support into the experience of those who have killed other people is essential because when they leave that setting—whether it's a war zone, a crime scene, or an accident location—they're going to return to their families. Those families often have as much disequilibrium as the identified patient does. We'll be dealing with some of those issues as well.

Understand when the process of forgiveness therapy and grief resolution are beneficial (and when they can be contraindicated)

Understanding how and where forgiveness can be beneficial or can be contraindicated is key.

As a minister, co-author Richard Nongard was trained in forgiveness. Forgiveness is the heart of many of our world religions. In the world of addiction counseling, most clients Richard saw who had taken a life did so because they had done something wrong. They had gotten high or drunk, and they had, with malevolence or impulsivity, taken somebody's life with a weapon, or in an automobile accident, or in other strange scenarios and situations. They truly were guilty. In fact, a court had actually adjudicated most of Richard's early substance abuse treatment clients as guilty. It's natural and appropriate to work with those individuals to help them experience forgiveness—self-forgiveness, societal forgiveness, and spiritual or metaphysical forgiveness.

After 2001, Richard began working with clients who had returned from a variety of military-related experiences, and their experiences in killing were entirely different. Forgiveness work was contraindicated, especially in the case of police officers or soldiers.

Because our society's view of killing, we expect that if you have killed somebody, then you must somehow be broken or upset about it, demoralized or guilty and depressed.

However, for a client who has a very strong identification with their role as a police officer or a soldier, they may not have any issue with that at all. Then if they're suddenly encouraged to experience these forgiveness processes, they may start doubting their own role, and the processes that were meant to help may take away a bit of their foundation. They may not feel they have any reason to forgive themselves.

Recognize the role of co-occurring PTSD and suicidal ideation, and examine tools to address each

As a new generation of warriors return back to the homeland, this is becoming a very significant issue within the Veterans Administration, within the military itself, and certainly within our communities.

However, we're not going to focus solely on the needs of the military community. We're going to be talking about post-traumatic stress disorder that could have emergence in any type of scenario or situation that meets the criteria. This insight is very important as we enter our twelfth year of being a nation at war with returning veterans each and every year.

Likewise, we need to recognize that not every returning soldier has PTSD. For that reason, we'll be examining recent changes to the Diagnostic and Statistical Manual.

A large portion of this book is dedicated to teaching specific approaches and intervention techniques. Many of these have applications far beyond working with those clients who have taken lives, and of course, there are certainly methods other than ours that may be helpful. However, at the end of this book, our readers should have a firm foundation to draw on when working with this uniquely challenging population.

THE FACE OF A KILLER

They drew near the house and a little old woman walked up to Dorothy, made a low bow and said, "You are welcome, most noble sorceress, to the land of the Munchkins. We are so grateful to you for having killed the Wicked Witch of the East and setting our people free from bondage."

What could she possibly mean by calling Dorothy a sorceress? And she had never killed anything. "You are very kind, but there must be some mistake. I have not killed anything," said Dorothy.

"Your house did anyway," said the old woman with a laugh, "and see, that is much the same thing."

Dorothy looked and gave a cry of fright. There under the corner of the house, two feet were sticking out shod in silver shoes.

"That's all that's left of the Wicked Witch of the East. She enslaved all the Munchkins for many years. Now they are free and very grateful to you for the favor."

— An excerpt from "The Wizard of Oz" by J. Frank Baum

We often think that we know what the face of a killer is—something scary, inhuman, a strange creature nothing like ourselves—and yet,

Dorothy and Toto begin their adventures in Oz by killing someone. Perhaps it could be considered justifiable manslaughter or accidental death, but in any case, we have to realize that those who have taken another life are not as different from us as we might suppose.

In fact, when we look at a list of celebrities who have actually taken the lives of others, we can see how common this is.

1. Laura Bush

In 1963, Laura Bush took the life of another driver when she failed to yield at a stop sign. Our former First Lady, Laura Bush, was one of those people who had actually taken a life.

2. Matthew Broderick

The eminently likable star of the movies *Ladyhawke* and *Ferris Bueller's Day Off*—a comedian, a fun-loving guy, an awesome actor—took the life of another person in a car accident. He was driving on a road in Ireland, had a head-on collision, and actually caused the death of another person.

There are so many different ways and reasons why people take other people's lives. Sometimes they're accidents, as in the first two cases. Then sometimes it happens through malevolence.

3. Adlai Stevenson

Adlai E. Stevenson was an ambassador, Vice-President, governor of Illinois, and candidate for President of the United States.

When Adlai Stevenson was twelve years old, he actually killed his childhood friend with an accidental gunshot.

4. Sid Vicious

The rock star Sid Vicious stabbed Nancy Vicious to death. That did not change any of his music, but it did change how people thought about his music.

5. Jason Williams

Jason Williams, an NBA player, was responsible for an accidental shooting.

6. Don King

Don King, the famous and flamboyant boxing promoter, has actually been convicted of two murders.

7. John Kerry

Former presidential candidate, senator for Massachusetts, and decorated Vietnam War veteran, John Kerry killed people in the line of duty.

8. Presidents Obama, Bush, Clinton, and Trump

Actually, every president of the United States, every chief of police, every platoon leader has had to make a decision that causes the death of other people. Even though they didn't pull the trigger and even though they didn't make the decision to engage in this behavior or that behavior, they still feel a sense of responsibility for the deaths that were caused by the decisions that they made.

9. Dr. Jack Kevorkian

The controversial "suicide doctor" of course took the lives of many people who had asked him to. He regarded it as a form of mercy killing, but others called it murder.

How many people have killed other people?

Though it's difficult to have an accurate statistic, we can estimate that about one out of every two hundred people has taken a life—our next-door neighbors, people whom we share a ride to work with, our colleagues and coworkers. If you work in a building with four hundred employees, it's statistically likely that two of those people have taken the life of another person.

If you're living in the city with 20,000 people, one hundred of those people have probably taken the life of somebody else. This is not an uncommon phenomenon.

Each year, about two hundred law enforcement officers in our country take the life of another person. Some of those incidents are accidents. Some occur with malevolence. The vast majority of these incidents happen in order to save other lives. Whatever the cause, about two hundred law enforcement officers each year take the life of others during the course of duty.

There are about 17,000 murders per year in the United States.

About 25,000 people die each year in drunk-driving related accidents. Sometimes that's the drunk driver, but sometimes it's a sober or inebriated passenger or other driver. Can you imagine sobering up to discover that you had taken the life of another person in a car accident? This statistic also includes drunk people who walk into oncoming traffic. Can you consider the guilt carried by a relatively safe, sober driver who runs over someone to drunk to stay out of harm's way?

There are about 4,500 workplace deaths per year. Some of those are self-inflicted: Suicide is the ultimate two-week notice. Some of those are accidental; it's possible to cause your own death by accident. Workplace violence is also an issue. More disturbing are industrial or construction workplace accidents in which one worker inadvertently causes the death of a coworker or colleague.

Despite how surprisingly common this phenomenon is, it's not something we talk about. It is something that in polite conversation we don't discuss at dinner.

Co-author David Parke has lived this. When the six-year-old child of one of David's friends met him, the father said, "And Dave is a soldier." So the six-year-old kid said, "Wow, are you a *real* soldier?" What the six-year-old kid was actually asking was, "Have you killed somebody?" In a six-year-old mind, that's what a real soldier does. Although the kid asked in a politically correct way, the politically incorrect question was just asked.

Because this is not an issue we discuss at dinner, it often becomes a topic for therapy and counseling, which is why we're presenting this book. We are going to share with you some specific methods for engaging the client in your office. We're going to provide you with therapeutic, spiritual, psychological, and metaphysical processes that you can utilize with clients who have killed other people.

Philosophy
and Background

PRESUPPOSITIONS

When we counsel those who have taken a life, we have to recognize that there are a lot of different reasons and situations involving clients have killed other people. They fall into four categories:

1. those who have killed by accident or negligence
2. those who have killed in the line of duty (police officers, soldiers)
3. those who have killed with malevolence
4. those who have killed in self-defense

It's very easy as therapists to project our own expectations onto our clients, so it's important to examine our presuppositions when we do this kind of work. We have found these presuppositions to be the most effective when serving those who have killed:

1. There is not a "correct" response to having killed another.
2. There is no universal response to killing others.
3. Psychological resilience exists in most people.
4. Each client will manifest unique responses.
5. Society will "time-bind" the act of killing others, even though society does not "time-bind" other situations that create remorse, grief, or guilt.

No "Correct" Response

As we look at the presuppositions that therapists have in working with clients who have killed other people, we have to recognize a couple of things. One, there is not a correct response from the client to having killed another person. There isn't a right or wrong response: "You should feel this way" or "You should not feel this way." It is simply the way they are.

As therapists, we're still humans. We have our own set of presuppositions of how people should feel and how they should respond, often based on what we would do and feel in our own frame of reference.

When clients who have taken the life of other people see us for therapy, we've seen a wide variety of different responses from the client. Some of those actually make no rational sense to us.

One client had, in self-defense, taken the life of another person. He did exactly what any reasonable person would do. In fact, many people in the community viewed him as a hero for having taken that action and saved himself. Yet his response to it was guilt, grief, and remorse.

Working in the criminal justice system, Richard has seen clients who should feel guilt, grief, and remorse—but they say, "Yeah, I took someone's life. So what? It didn't matter anyway. Neither does my life." It's often shocking how different the response is from what we thought the response should be.

In doing therapy with people who have killed other people, we have to recognize that there is no *correct* response. There simply is the response that our client has.

No Universal Response

The next presupposition, which is very similar, is there's no universal response to killing others.

When a thirty-two-year-old client was rear-ended at a stoplight, his car went forward and hit a pedestrian, killing her. What was interesting about it was his response to the situation: Although he did feel remorse in a very general sense, but he did not really feel it personally. His response was, "I've always wondered what it would be like to kill another person. Here I have, not through my own actions or through my own hand, but technically I did it." For him, it was almost like a task that had been accomplished in some way.

Sometimes soldiers have a similar feeling: It's almost a rite of passage. It's a part of the role for a lot of soldiers. David can vouch that, especially in the special operations community, a soldier could have achieved everything possible in the military, but may feel as though until he takes that next step, until he actually kills an enemy in combat, he has not fulfilled his job. He has not fulfilled his role as a defender of our nation.

Psychological Resilience

The third presupposition is really contrary to what we as therapists are often taught. The fact is that people are psychologically resilient. The vast majority of people who take the life of another person are not sick and pathological. Psychological resilience is the normal state of humans. As therapists, we often forget that.

So when we have somebody who has taken the life of another person, particularly when we're dealing with service members, police officers—those who act in self-preservation in the line of duty—as therapists we say, "There must be some sort of pathological response here."

Obviously we've become much more aware of these things. But when half the service members are coming back with a diagnosis, we have to ask whether we have created a social scenario or situation where this is the expected response?

This is partly a social contagion issue. When we stop treating somebody as if they're resilient and as if they can handle it, then we're creating a secondary gain to the situation. There is a lot of benefit to being the broken killer whether that's an inmate or a soldier. There's a lot of benefit to that in our society, the way people treat that individual.

It's amazing how we've really lost sight of psychological resilience as being the norm. We prepare people for the impending diagnosis. Just as an athletic trainer should help an athlete to become strong, we need to teach psychological resilience to those who serve our country or community.

Soldiers get bombarded with the suicide prevention classes right up front, which is basically telling them, "There's going to be something wrong with you at some point. When it does go wrong, this is how you handle it."

It's a dilemma. We want soldiers and other people to have the resources, so that when they need help, they can take advantage of it. But at the same time, we don't want to lose sight of a basic presupposition of effective counseling: that our clients are remarkably resilient. Fortunately, people are resilient. That is a strength that we can tap into in the problem-solving process.

Unique Responses

The fourth presupposition is that each client will manifest unique responses. When we're sitting with somebody who has killed, our job is to be expansive and accepting as possible.

We can guide our clients, but we must do it carefully. In fact, if we're not careful, we can actually manipulate them, even unconsciously, to respond to the event in the way that we see fit. So if we don't create a really wide-open and very clean space for them to work through how they actually feel about it themselves, then we're really doing our clients a disservice.

Time-Binding

The last presupposition is really interesting; it's based on sociology rather than psychology.

Society time-binds the killing of another person. Society doesn't time-bind other situations that create remorse, guilt, or grief—but when an individual has taken another person's life, they are *always* the person who's taken another person's life. They're always a killer, always a murderer. It's a label—an identity—they carry forever. We'd like to see it change so we can actually let people live a new identity rather than being stuck with that old identity.

Notice how if your parent passes away, you're not always an orphan. If you get divorced, you're not *always* a divorcee. In the 1920s you were, as this story illustrates:

In 1982, Richard's father passed away, making him the last male Nongard alive for a while other than his old Uncle Conrad, who was 90. At Richard's father's funeral, old Uncle Conrad called the seventeen-year-old Richard over and said, "I have something I need to tell you."

Richard answered, "Okay."

He said, "Something important."

Richard repeated, "Okay."

He said, "You need to know…" Richard wondered if Uncle Conrad was about to tell where the buried treasure was.

He continued, "Before your grandfather was married to your grandmother, he was married to someone else."

Richard said, "Okay."

He said, "They got divorced."

Richard said, "Okay."

"Nobody knows this."

"Did they have kids?" Richard asked.

"No," answered Uncle Conrad.

"I don't have to share the inheritance with anybody?"

"No," said the old man, "but I wanted you to know this."

He had kept this family secret for 60 years because Richard's grandfather and grandmother were always divorcees to him and to their society, whereas now we joke around about how many times we've been married or having a starter marriage. Culture has really changed.

But it's a different matter for those who have taken the life of another person. They always carry the stigma. People say or think: *That's the soldier who killed those people. That's the officer in the department who killed those people. That's the bus driver who took that life. That's the neighbor who accidentally shot the kid when he was cleaning his guns.*

Somebody with a criminal background cannot even apply for a job without disclosing his or her crime. Therefore, they are time-bound by whatever decisions, by whatever choices, by whatever actions they made in the past.

As therapists, this is important to us because we have to recognize that in trying to integrate our client into a role of what we would call equilibrium, we're going to be dealing with this cultural aspect of counseling the client who has taken the life of other people.

A lot of times we need to focus on things that are not centered actually around the killing, to focus on the other resourceful areas of their life or whatever else will break down that time-binding and move them past that.

Applying these Presuppositions

How does this translate into what you can do as a therapist with the clients in your office? How have the things we touched on so far important in either the assessment process or in the therapeutic process with clients?

It's important as a therapist to create that space for the client to come in with a very unique situation. They're going to feel a lot of pressure from society in general to feel a particular way, and a lot of times they're going to feel conflict.

We have these models society lives by. This goes specifically for police officers and soldiers, but it can filter across. Somehow the good guy is supposed to win by being good. Somehow the good guy is inherently more skillful and victorious based on the virtue of being good.

On television shows like *The Lone Langer* or the *A-Team*, the heroes never killed anybody. The Lone Ranger always shot the guns out of the bad guy's hands, but never killed the bad guy. He was always able to shoot the gun out of their hands. There's this idea that there's something wrong if you kill somebody, and you must feel a particular way about it.

In our society, we think, "They killed somebody. They must feel horrible."

At one of our live workshops, one of the therapists who was attending said that she had a client who was a soldier in Afghanistan and had killed a number of people during combat, did his job very well, and didn't feel bad about it. But now he considers himself a monster for not feeling bad about it when he was doing it. He still doesn't feel bad about it. What he feels bad about is not feeling bad about it.

Now that she understands that, she has a whole new level she can work with him on, exploring why he should feel bad now and what it means to have not felt bad while he was doing that, as opposed to just saying, "You're not a monster because you killed those people." He didn't think he was a monster for killing the people.

In short, we have to strive to really understand the client's model of the world as opposed to the societal model or our own personal models.

RELIGIOUS AND CULTURAL FRAMES

Whether you're religious or not, whether your client is religious or not, how we perceive things is often filtered through a frame of our culture's religious ideas. We could easily do an entire book on religious frames and cultural frames of taking another person's life, but even this brief overview will illustrate the variety of perspectives that may affect your client.

In the United States, we usually see things from a European Judeo-Christian perspective. That's probably the dominant paradigm that most of our readers use as a cultural lens or frame of reference.

But we need to remember that there are many different religious viewpoints throughout the world that shape our understanding of taking another person's life. Some of these certainly pre-date Christianity. In fact, each society's attempt to understand human behavior has really built to the point where we are today.

Let's look at the Bhagavad-Gita. Why is that relevant to this discussion?

The Bhagavad-Gita is very interesting. It's a small section of a larger work, the Mahabharata, which is an Indian epic that Brahmanism or Hinduism uses as scripture. The Bhagavad-Gita is smaller chapter of that, or a smaller book of it.

The whole book takes place on a battlefield. The protagonist, Arjuna, is set to fight in defense of his kingdom against another army, but the other army is full of his cousins and uncles—people whom he loves, people who have raised him, people who have taught him—who are not bad people.

He's really caught up in this sense of existential angst and spiritual malaise about the whole thing and would really rather not fight. His chariot driver happens to be Krishna, who is the avatar of the god Vishnu, and Krishna basically guides him by saying, "It's your dharma, your path. You have to fight this battle."

The work is the philosophical conversation between them, in which Krishna explains that death is not an ending, because life and death are twin sides of an illusion. He describes death as a matter of the immortal soul laying down a body the way that we take off our clothes at the end of the day. Thus he says it's impossible to really kill, because you can't kill the immortal soul, which is calls the "Self" in this translation:

Only the material bodies of the Self are subject to destruction, it is said, while the Self itself is indestructible, immeasurable and eternal. Fight therefore, O descendant of Bharata. (2.18)

One who takes the Self to be the slayer and the one who thinks He is slain, neither of them knows; The Self slays not nor is He slain. (Bhagavad Gita 2.19)

One who knows this Self to be indestructible, eternal, unborn and immutable, O Partha, how can that person slay or cause to be slain. (2.21)

Its impact in our culture is in the military where we seek justification for war and justification for taking the life of others.

The ancient Hindu text addresses essentially the art of war and how to deal with the emotional aspects of it. The Old Testament—the Jewish Torah—also gives a justification for war:

Do not say in your heart, after the Lord your God has thrust them out before you, 'It is because of my righteousness that the Lord has brought me in to possess this land,' whereas it is because of the wickedness of these nations that the Lord is driving them out before you. Not because of your righteousness or the uprightness of your heart are you going in to possess their land, but because of the wickedness of these nations the Lord your God is driving them out from before you, and that he may confirm the word that the Lord swore to your fathers, to Abraham, to Isaac, and to Jacob. Know, therefore, that the Lord your God is not giving you this good land to possess because of your righteousness, for you are a stubborn people. (Deuteronomy 9: 4-6)

The New Testament also comments on violence:

Then Jesus said to him, "Put your sword back into its place. For all who take the sword will perish by the sword." (Matthew 26:52)

The apostle Paul comments on the role of violence in law enforcement:

Let every person be subject to the governing authorities. For there is no authority except from God, and those that exist have been instituted by God. Therefore whoever resists the authorities resists what God has appointed, and those who resist will incur judgment. For rulers are not a terror to good conduct, but to bad. Would you have no fear of the one who is in authority? Then do what is good, and you will receive his approval, for he is God's servant for your good. But if you do wrong, be afraid, for he does not bear the sword in vain. For he is the servant of God, an avenger who carries out God's wrath on the wrongdoer. Therefore one must be in subjection, not only to avoid God's wrath but also for the sake of conscience. (Romans 13:1-7)

All of these things shape our understanding. The Quran addresses the topic as well:

Then fight in the cause of Allah, and know that Allah heareth and knoweth all things. (2:244)

Fighting is prescribed for you, and ye dislike it. But it is possible that ye dislike a thing which is good for you, and that ye love a thing which is bad for you. But Allah knoweth, and ye know not. (2:216)

In other words, often our justification for the ability to take another person's life is there's something bigger going on than you understand. You are merely playing your part, your role—which is, by the way, one of the reasons why from these cultural understandings, the soldier can take the action that's required for their job, or the police officer can, or any other professional who is defending (or at least perceives himself to be defending) the interest of others who cannot defend themselves.

Because of this, in many military units and organizations, fighters do not wrestle with having to take a life while in the service. It is a very accepted role, and typically, a volunteer role.

Richard has a brother-in-law who is a sheriff's deputy and who spent ten years as an infantryman, serving primarily in Iraq and Afghanistan. After watching the video this book is based on, he said, "Wow, that information was really useful to me as a former soldier. I wish that we had this information in boot camp. I wish we had that ahead of time."

Even though the soldiers in the unit at the time didn't wrestle with it, Richard's brother-in-law, who is probably representative of a lot of infantrymen who have done their job well and taken the lives of other individuals, after the fact said, "I wasn't prepared to acknowledge to my fellow soldiers that this was an issue I dealt with."

We have to know when a soldier deals with it what specific aspect of it they're dealing with. Society as a whole thinks it's all about the killing, saying, "You took a life; therefore, there's something you have to do or feel about it."

They think it's about the traumatic event that occurred. A mortar was coming at you. You fired. That was the right thing to do. So people ask, "How do you feel about the PTSD from almost being blown up?"

If there were a universal response to killing, to having been in war, then you would think that we would have heard about all the broken Vikings or all the Samurai—but we don't. These warrior cultures really honored that role or aspect, rather than expecting people to be broken.

Because we live in a very conscientious society, because we live in a very humanistic society, we hear certain messages about human life: "Every life is a gift" and "All life has value." We're not saying that's true or not true. What we're saying is that we have to be aware that constant message informs our whole society.

Then when somebody has been the actor, the person who took the life no matter what role they were in, now society focuses in on that and asks, "Are you okay?" Then when somebody asks them that question, they do the internal derivative search. They look for the answer. "*Am* I okay? I hadn't thought about it." It's interesting. A lot of them may come to the conclusion, "No, I'm not okay."

What we have to take into account is that many of these people weren't okay before they took a life. That's certainly one of the issues that is at play as well.

So when we see a soldier who comes back from conflict having significant difficulties, we have to ask ourselves whether the conflict caused the difficulty, or did the lack of psychological resilience that preceded the situation cause the difficulty. We don't necessarily know the answer to that. But we do know that many people who were firemen and police officers on September 11, 2001, didn't manifest post-traumatic stress disorder, yet others did.

What is the difference? They were at the same event. They have the same experience. A big part of that was the psychological resources, resilience, propensity, knowledge, and skills that they had preceding the event.

There could be biology involved, too. Socialization could be an issue. We don't know the answer, but we still have to ask: Does the current wartime generation have less resilience than past generations? Are we raising children today with less resilience than the children that were raised before? Are we creating problems by expecting problems, or are we creating problems by failing to prepare for them?

Whatever the cause of your client's reactions to having taken a life, it's important to consider the religious and cultural narrative that may be shaping your client's thoughts on the matter.

THE PRAXEOLOGICAL APPROACH

The praxeological needs of people who have killed other people can be divided into eight categories. As we discussed earlier, the word *praxeological* means "all-encompassing." While we put these needs into eight categories, there could just as easily be eighty. However, these are as unique needs we've seen in those clients who have killed other people.

We'll discuss each of these at length:

1. Spiritual Congruence
2. Social Belonging
3. Psychological Flexibility
4. Physical Wellness
5. Acceptance
6. Mindful Living
7. Purposeful Living
8. Problem-Solving Skills

Spiritual Congruence

Let's define spiritual, because a lot of people mistake religion for spirituality. We're not talking about being in congruence with a religious faith or a dogma or a set of commandments. Our deepest needs on a spiritual level really are the need for security, the need for significance, the need for belonging, the need to love other people, and the need to feel worthy of receiving love in return.

If your client has taken someone's life, they may feel physically insecure because retribution could be in store for them. If your client has taken someone's life, they may feel unlovable because they believe they've done the most horrendous thing of all.

They may feel a lack of security because, in taking a life, they caused a change in the family structure or the financial structure of the family, and now the stability that was there is no longer there.

Likewise, personal significance is really affected by time-binding. Your client may ask, "How can I be a significant person when society judges my identity based on something I did in the past?"

Alternatively, clients may get their significance from being broken. If they were living with a low level of significance in their life and now they're getting all this attention or all these resources or emotional resources thrown their way, it can create a loop, a descending spiral, in which they become more and more broken by the idea of killing because now they've found a tool for significance in their life.

Obviously a person's religion can be an important part. Religion, no matter what religion it is, tries to impart a sense of security, a sense of significance, a sense of love, a sense of belonging, a sense of acceptance.

Aside from religion, how can we meet those spiritual needs? What processes are truly useful to a person? In what ways can we reinforce or help the client come into spiritual congruence?

People bring their childhood or religious presuppositions into their adult world, which goes back to a person's own spiritual model. We really have to have an in-depth understanding of what their spiritual model is. Are they Christian? If they are Christian, do they feel they're going to go to hell for killing or are they justified because David killed Goliath? Jesus was the messenger of love, but what does that mean to your client?

If they're Buddhist or Hindu, what are the karmic ramifications of killing?

Really, we have to have a fundamental understanding of their world view and what childhood presuppositions they may be bringing into their adult world. Ask, "What does God or the Universe say, feel, or think about the action that you've taken?

That's a great question. One thing to love about solution-focused brief therapy is its dependence on questions. Most people know solution-focused brief therapy from the miracle question: "If a miracle were to happen in the middle of the night and you were to wake up in the morning and your problem was resolved, how would you know it was resolved? You just woke up and you're lying in your bed. How would you know it was resolved?"

That's a great question. The questioning approach to therapy is very effective. Sometimes we have fun with that a little bit: "So, how do you feel? So, how did you feel when you felt the feeling that you felt? So, you felt the feeling that you felt when you felt the feeling—how did that feel?"

Whether it was Milton Erickson chunking down or whether it was Virginia Satir chunking up, a questioning approach is important.

One thing we tell people is to separate the spiritual needs from religion. Some of Richard's former minister associates might not like that process, but it's psychologically beneficial to your client to let them see that while security, significance, acceptance, love, belonging can be met through religion—or through a relationship with a higher power or God of their understanding—all of those needs can be met by developing resource states.

You have the ability to generate within you resource states – those states that are resourceful to you and problem solving. Here is a process that focuses on one of those, that being security:

In just a moment, I'll ask you to close your eyes. Before you do, notice how you are easily breathing in and out, and then think about how by reading this book, you are preparing to do a fantastic job for your clients. You might even be preparing to earn CEU hours by reading this book, and that's important.

What that means is you don't have to worry about whether or not you'll get your CEUs done in time or whether or not you'll have to pay a late penalty fee or whether or not you'll accrue the hours that are necessary by the time you need to renew your license.

So because of what you're doing right now, you could actually feel a sense of security in that area of your life. There may be more to do, but you're actively and actually doing what you need to right at this moment.

Also, because you are reading this book, you are preparing yourself to work with the kind of clients that some people might think are difficult. You, on the other hand, can feel prepared, confident in your ability to help people who need it. This can develop as a sense of security in your own abilities as a therapist.

Note what it feels like to have that security, the feeling of security with every breath, breathe in. Security of this situation and aspect of your life. Become familiar with security, letting yourself feel the sense of security and now amplify that sense of security. Breathe in a breath amplifying that sense of security, breathing in another breath, letting yourself feel the experience of security. Go ahead and close your eyes and continue to explore and expand that feeling of security for just a short while.

That was a real simple, basic one-minute process where you created an experience of identifying what security in a situation feels like, and then recognizing your own ability to amplify that state. You were able to do it, with each breath feeling more secure in that situation. Doesn't it feel awesome to know that you're doing exactly what you need to be doing?

Although this certainly is not nearly as serious of an issue as having taken the life of another person, if we can create a sense of security, which is a spiritual need, through a process of awareness and amplification in this less significant area of life, we apply that same model to a significant area of life. We can utilize these processes with clients to let them see that they have within them the resources necessary to develop a spiritual congruence.

One other way to emphasize spiritual congruence is to really help somebody approach themselves with a sense of gentleness and unconditional friendship.

A lot of times what we may do when a client is being particularly hard on themselves is take the content of their expression and place it in a new context: "What if your brother, your best friend, your father, your mother, your sister or whoever else had done this thing? Would you be as hard on them? Would you say the same things to them that you're saying to yourself?"

It really isolates how they're treating themselves as opposed to how they would treat the rest of their world.

Social Belonging

How do we go about helping a person who has taken the life of another person create a sense of social belonging?

Often they feel that they have a scarlet letter, a "K" for Killer, on their forehead. Everybody is going to know that. They saw it on the evening news or the Internet. They put a picture of the city bus and a picture of the bus driver on the evening news. Everyone who gets on the bus is going to know.

People really think that they stand out from the crowd when they've taken the life of another person. What processes can we use with a client to help them create a sense of social belonging when they feel disconnected from society?

There are two aspects to social belonging:

1. if a person does feel like they have that "K" on their forehead
2. if society itself is putting that on them, and they don't feel it

There's the internal model and the external model.

A lot of times with social belonging, a person feels as though "I'm different because I have killed." That's an internal model. In order to point out that society is not necessarily treating them that way, we can point out any other difference that they have with society or the bulk of people.

David is bald. If his focus were on being bald, then he would walk around and interpret every activity or every behavior that came in his direction through that lens, through that filter. One of the things is to help a person identify what people are focusing on. Even if people are focusing on the fact that David is bald, he can choose not to focus on it. He doesn't let that become his identity.

It may take a process and some practice to get them to where they treat having killed somebody as just a casual event. If they don't identify with that any more than they identify with their twelfth-grade report card, that it was an event that happened (fortunate or unfortunate), it ceases to be an issue.

For social belonging, help your clients find the people they do socially belong to. It may not be a group of similar people.

We're not necessarily recommending support groups here, because in support groups, the topic of conversation and the emphasis seems to be on maintaining an identity, and maintaining an identity time-binds us. If your clients feel more comfortable socializing with police officers or they feel more comfortable with other soldiers or whatever else, it's fine to be around them, but not necessarily in a support group way.

What we're trying to do is normalize their life, rather than segregate them by issue, rather than assign an identity: "My name is ______. I killed someone." And that's what they are for the rest of my life. That becomes their identity.

We have to consider the "What am I?" that is not this: "What am I that is not a killer? I'm not just a bus driver who killed somebody or a kid who was careless with a gun or a drunk driver. I am ______."

The more we define something, the more we limit all other possibilities. If my identity becomes so tightly bound around being a killer as opposed to that just being one of a thousand facets of me, it gets diluted when I take it into the spectrum of all of that I am.

Social belonging becomes a matter of their frame and what they're going to focus on. A lot of times in a social setting, most of what happens is due to our own filters. If you change your filters, you will inherently change your sense of belonging.

Psychological Flexibility

Our clients are resilient, but often lack psychological flexibility. By psychological flexibility, we're talking about what Albert Ellis meant when he discussed high frustration tolerance. What's one way that we can increase our clients' tolerance of stressful emotions and feelings?

Psychological flexibility is one of those traits that helps a person to succeed in the long run. So if your client has killed somebody and feels an intense psychological and spiritual guilt or an intense depression or anxiety, what are some ways that we can approach clients to help them develop some flexibility?

Whereas in the past they may have viewed things from an absolute perspective, a black-and-white perspective, we can scale our clients' experiences into a relative perspective. When a client says, "I'm depressed," you can say, "On a scale of 1-10, how depressed are you?" That's probably one of the simple strategies, but we have found it to be the most effective because our clients, up until we asked them, were either depressed OR happy. They were either anxious OR confident. They're either this OR that—not angry at a level 2, or angry at a level 6, or angry at a level 7, or angry at a level 10.

Another thing to do with depressed clients is to ask them, "Are you always depressed? When you're in the shower, are you depressed? When you're going to the bathroom, are you depressed?" If you can make them laugh or make them angry, ask, "Well, you're angry right now. Are you depressed?"

They might answer, "No, I'm just pissed off at you!"

"Okay, good. So you're not full-time depressed; you're part-time depressed. Now we just need to figure out what needs to happen for you to become depressed when you're depressed part-time."

We've had clients who say, "I've always been depressed." We have clients who have been depressed for so long that they have a hard time remembering a time when they weren't depressed. So we'll ask them, "Do you have an old photo? Go through your old pictures. Do you have some pictures from a year ago, or five years ago, or ten years ago? Look at your Facebook page. Look at your pictures on there over the last couple of years. Go dig out your MySpace pictures and go back some years ago. Look at those pictures."

Facebook is really a cool invention because we can actually see the pictures right there in the office. We can go through their pictures and find a picture where they look happy.

We'll say, "You look happy."

"Yeah, I was happy. That was my eighth birthday party. My friends were there. I got a walkie-talkie set for my birthday. That was the last time I was happy."

"So you weren't always depressed."

They weren't born that way, and we can use those questions and photos to really break the misbelief of "I've always been that way." None of us can always be the same way always. It's not possible.

Another part of psychological flexibility that's really important is the idea of what creates our suffering. Albert Ellis talks about this with "shoulding" ourselves to death and "musterbation."

What creates suffering is the shoulds that we have in our mind, our second order of reality, the way we believe. I call the objective world—what happens out here—first order reality, and the events I experience after they pass through my filters as second order reality. But my second order reality is far more real than first order reality. It's all that I really experience.

There are four questions to ask clients:

What does that mean?

If it's about "I killed somebody," what does that mean? They'll tell you. What this essentially does is give you their model of the world.

How do you know that's true?

We really can't know anything is true. This question is going to help develop their model more fully, but it also will start to put little breaks in their thinking, because everybody knows that you can't *really* know in a lot of ways.

What else can it mean?

This is the big thing. It's something they've never considered before. Even if you're dealing with an ex-convict who says, "I'm a horrible person because I killed these people," or "I was hardcore and getting respect, so I'm glad because I was a man because I killed these people." Ask, "So it means you're a man because you were killing these people. How do you know that's true?" Then they say, "That's basically what my culture was, my society was, my ______ was." That's what his world was then. What else could it mean?

Psychological flexibility is needed not only in a person who has a very uncertain map. It can help create uncertainty in a state where they're certain—but it's not a beneficial sense of certainty for them. Flexibility can help create a little bit of uncertainty to find a new avenue that might be more beneficial.

What's the most beneficial meaning?

That's the one they can pick. Which meaning is actually the most beneficial? It is really the same thing as having a client say, "What else can I do?" Ask your clients to pick the one they'd be willing to do. Now we have a healthy action. Now we have a healthy belief. In this case, we've gained the ability to flex our psychology.

If I ask, "What does it mean?" they have already told me the meaning typically. What would it mean if you could find other people who have done this? In the case of killing, do you watch action movies? Who is your favorite action star? In his action movies, did he ever kill anybody? What did it mean when he killed him?

You can model other people, fictional or real people. It doesn't matter. For somebody who won a Congressional Medal of Honor, what did killing mean? What did it mean when Sergeant York killed people?

Create a list of how many other meanings. Flexibility is a matter of choice, a matter of options. The fewer choices you have, the fewer options you have, and the less flexibility you have.

One of our favorite questions in therapy has always been, "What else could you do?"

Clients often think, "Well, there isn't anything else I could do or I would've done."

Psychological flexibility is vital for not just this topic, but for anything.

Physical Wellbeing

When people have experienced crisis, they often put aside their own physical needs. They stop sleeping. They're not necessarily eating right.

A person can only function emotionally as well as they are physically. People need to take care of themselves physically in order to function emotionally.

What are some ways that we can encourage our clients other than simply asking them, "Are you eating right? Are you sleeping right?" What can we do to actually help our clients meet their physical needs as they begin to address what are some pretty difficult emotional issues for them?

You're probably already familiar with the idea that exercise is like the big guns when it comes to depression.

We talk about psychotropics being so effective, even though the research is really a little mixed on that (but that's for another book). But one of the things we do know is that cardiovascular exercise three times a week for 45 minutes or longer is twice as effective at alleviating the symptoms of major depression than psychotropic medication.

And yet, the psychiatrist's first intervention with clients is also to write a prescription rather than to look at if the person is actually engaging in those activities that have proven to be most effective.

A lot of the work for this comes from a gentleman named Dr. BJ Fogg. He does work at Stanford and started their persuasion lab. He originally started out working with computers and how computers could influence people. But since then he's become much more involved in other areas of influence.

If we were to say, "Working out is good for you," and they say they're going to work out and they don't—they just can't seem to muster the idea—the best strategy is to create a series of easily achievable goals. The confidence that's attained from achieving a simple goal, whether it's working out or eating right or anything else like that, provides a boost for reaching the next goal.

People think physical activity means going to the gym. Some of our clients are so depressed that physical activity may simply mean getting up and walking out the front door of the house. We're going to adjust this to our client's level. Not every client needs to join the gym in order to take care of their mental health, but people do need to become active.

Do you remember the movie *What About Bob?* Richard Dreyfus played the psychiatrist, and Bill Murray played Bob. The psychiatrist had written a book called *Baby Steps*. This is the same idea. If we say, "Go to the gym," then client says, "That's another overwhelming task I can't do." But getting up each morning and stepping out of the house may be easier.

We tell our clients, "Even if stepping out of the house is overwhelming for the client, the first morning or the first week, just put on your shoes. You don't have to go anywhere. You don't have to do anything. Just put on your shoes."

We build each time on the idea of the next measurable accomplishment. What's the next measurable step that we can take?

It's very important that we monitor the client's "should" view of the world, their second order reality, because we don't want them beating themselves up over the fact that they can't leave the house. We want to ego-strengthen to the point of, "It's okay. This is just where you're at right now. So for the next five days, I just want you to put on shoes. For the next five days, I want you just to eat an apple. One apple or one piece of broccoli."

In BJ Fogg's own stories, he talks about how for him flossing was the mountain he could not climb, so he committed to just flossing one tooth a day. He set it up so that each day he would make sure that his floss was right by his toothbrush.

With your clients, they may want to put their shoes right by the bed, right by the TV, somewhere where it's convenient. They don't even have to go to the closet to get them, but they're in the same place to make it a very simple task for them to do.

Let's talk about sleep as it relates to physical wellness because we think of physical wellness as exercise and eating and not smoking and those sorts of things.

Some of those things are maybe the big guns that may be tools for relapse prevention. As hypnosis practitioners, we're big advocates of smoking cessation, but when a client comes in with distress related to having killed somebody, quitting smoking is going to be way down the list of things to impact first. It's not that it's going to be healthy for them to smoke. It actually contributes to depression, but for the time being, it's best to leave that alone.

Sleep is one of those things you really should assess. You've probably noticed in your own life that your ability to relate to people in the world and your ability to communicate your ideas, to do your job, to feel good about yourself is really in direct proportion to how much sleep you got the night before.

We ask our clients a lot about their sleeping. Sometimes we actually have to teach clients to sleep. What's interesting is there are some techniques that are really useful. One of those techniques is simply progressive muscle relaxation and self-hypnosis.

Hypnos is actually the Greek word for sleep. There's probably nothing better for teaching a person to sleep. Just like a parent needs to teach a child how to self-soothe and put themselves to bed, sometimes we have an adult whom we need to teach that skill set to, and we can actually do that with self-hypnosis training.

There are other strategies that are really useful as well. For example, when we have clients who have reversed their days and their nights, they find it very distressing. They stay up until 5:00 or 6:00 in the morning often because their anxiety and their obsessive thoughts about events that are distressing to them keep them awake until they physically can't stay awake anymore. Then they sleep until the crack of noon or 2:00 or 4:00 in the afternoon. They become distressed that their days and nights are flipped around.

The strategy for resolving this is pretty interesting. Instead of trying to get them to go to bed earlier, we actually try to get them to go to bed later working around the clock. So if they stay up until 5:00 every morning, now we get them to stay up until 6:00, the next day until 7:00, the next day until 8:00, the next day until 9:00 and work themselves actually around the clock clockwise rather than counter-clockwise. It seems to be easier for some of our clients to then flip their days and nights. That's a strategy that can be effective.

One of the most effective strategies, in addition to self-hypnosis, is mindfulness. The reason why my clients can't sleep at night is often because when they turn the day off and lie in bed it's just them and their thoughts. We say more about this in the mindfulness chapter.

Acceptance

There's a famous passage in the *Big Book Alcoholics Anonymous*. It's better referred to as Page 449: "And acceptance is the answer to all my problems today."

A lot of people really struggle with that idea of acceptance. They ask, "You mean I have to like something awful?"

When we're directing a client who has killed somebody towards acceptance, we're not working with them towards accepting killing as either normal or wonderful or awesome or something they hope happens to them again or to other people.

By acceptance we really mean helping a client to recognize that what is simply is, and that acceptance is moving a client towards a point where they're simply able or willing to lay out on the table that which is and see it. They don't have to endorse it nor like it, but they have to simply acknowledge its existence.

Often, visualization exercises can help a person experience better than an explanation. Here is one such basic process:

Go ahead and close your eyes. By the time you're the age that we are in life, certainly there is an experience in your life which has been difficult for you, or something not only difficult but even unfortunate in your experiences. Identify that. Think of that.

So as you breathe in and breathe out in the safety of my office, imagine that space on the floor in front of us. Imagine that on the floor in front of us is a box. Imagine going to that box and opening that box and looking in that box and seeing the representations of those things which have been so difficult in the safety of my office.

Imagine the different items in that box. Identify what you see inside of that box. Now in the safety of the office, I'm here with you. Can you take one of those items out and place it on the floor here in my office? And even another one of those items, placing it on the floor here in the office. In fact, empty out the box letting all of those items simply be on the floor here in the office.

Now imagine sitting back in your chair being where you are and seeing those representations of that which is most difficult right there on the floor here in the office. Of course it doesn't mean we like it. It doesn't mean we want it here. It doesn't mean we wish that it would happen again, but we can simply see it here in the safety of the vantage point of this office.

As you breathe in and breathe out, be ready to open the eyes. Taking in a deep breath, opening the eyes, feeling energetic from that oxygen.

We abbreviated that process. With clients, we will actually have them visualize taking those representational objects out and putting them on that table, and even exiting the room and simply turning off the lights. They're still there. They can return to it anytime they wanted to for whatever reason—to be angry with that, to grieve, to whatever. But they simply acknowledge it.

Creating experiential scenarios for our clients can help them move towards a point of acceptance. Of course mindfulness plays into acceptance because when you're mindful, you are in the present, even if the event was in the past.

Acceptance is really an attitude of "it is what it is." A lot of people think that acceptance is difficult for clients. Yet we've seen that clients find relief in acceptance. When they understand what acceptance is, it's sort of like surrender. Those are two words that have a very distinct meaning in our culture, but really what we're looking for is not the same meaning that most people attribute to those words. Both acceptance and surrender are really empowering ideas that give us back control of our perceptions and our thoughts.

Rapport is very important, and that's why acceptance is important on the part of a therapist, too. If a client came into you because they bite their nails, you would not invest a lot emotionally into that; therefore, your rapport with that client would probably actually be pretty good because you're really there just accepting it.

In contrast, if you have a client who has killed with malevolence, it's easy to put too much emotional energy into that. We want to do good or we want to help this person or we are scared of the person or we feel this way or that way.

In the grand scheme of things and the ultimate operation of the universe, each issue is very similar to the other: It's an event that happened in the past that a person is having a problem dealing with.

If we can take that accepting attitude towards our clients, we are, in a way, teaching them. We model approval as their vehicle for acceptance of themselves.

At the beginning we said a lot of the traditional approaches actually cause difficulty. Instead of trying to get clients to become un-depressed, we're going to accept their depression. Too often, therapists try to get their clients un-traumatized in order to be better. We try to get them un-anxious. Acceptance simply says, "I'm anxious" or "I'm depressed."

When you accept your depression, when you accept your trauma, when you accept your anxiety, that acceptance paradoxically provides a sense of freedom. When you accept it, it no longer has power.

That's one of the beauties of paradoxical intent. If you haven't yet, read some Viktor Frankl and his paradoxical interventions with people. The idea is, "Hey, invite more of that problem in. Show me how much control you have over it."

Acceptance really makes the issue into a non-issue. Often we create more suffering through the attempt of solving our problem.

Following things through to their logical extreme is a technique of Albert Ellis. Imagine that you are feeling a lot of anxiety because you don't want to re-experience that event where you killed someone.

Suppose your client says something like this:

Client: I feel anxious.

Therapist: Okay. You said you feel anxious. What's the worst thing that could happen to you when you feel anxious?

> **Client:** I don't know. I could have a hard time breathing. I could lose sleep.
>
> **Therapist:** What's the worst thing that could happen if you have a hard time breathing?
>
> **Client:** I could pass out.
>
> **Therapist:** And if you pass out, what happens to your breathing?
>
> **Client:** It goes back to normal.

When we follow things through to their logical extreme, what we almost always find is that as long as we're breathing we're okay. We can use these techniques to assist our clients in the interviewing process of de-catastrophizing those things that they find produces so much anxiety.

Or you might take a Frank Farrelly provocative therapy approach:

> **Client:** I feel bad because I killed a person.
>
> **Therapist:** You killed one person?
>
> **Client:** Yeah.
>
> **Therapist:** Well, one person is not even that big of a deal. If you had come in and told me you killed fifty, then I might think that you had something to be concerned about.

That's provocative therapy, which is not a technique we'll use with every client. It's certainly not always appropriate. But it would be appropriate for some clients. It's the idea of testing.

In your own level of acceptance, know that each client has a different model of how they feel and how they respond to the world and what their subjective reality is, and take a playful attitude. We don't mean a funny or non-serious attitude. We don't mean an attitude that dismisses the client or the severity of their condition, but you yourself have this playful, curious attitude about what it is that this client needs most right now.

The NLP frame that relates to this is TOTE (test, operate, test, exit). It really goes "test, operate, test, operate, test, operate, test, until you find it, then exit." It doesn't have to be this one-shot fix all the time.

Often in the world of therapy our clients are looking for that pill that makes it better, the Holy Grail. In therapy, because of the constraints that give us limited time with our clients, we're looking for that technique which resolves everything. Really, it's a combination of all of these things that can be most effective and us being inquisitive enough to look for that which is going to be most effective.

Mindful Living

We're going to have a separate chapter on mindfulness exercises, but part of the praxeological approach is mindful living. This is the ultimate goal of mindfulness exercises.

That's what Jon Kabat-Zin teaches with mindfulness-based stress reduction and mindfulness meditation. The purpose of meditation is not to take twenty, thirty, or forty minutes sitting in a corner. The purpose of meditation is so that after mediation becomes who you are, you can meditate twenty-four hours a day.

It's a bit like sharpening an axe. When you're sharpening an axe, you're not actually chopping on a tree, but it makes it a heck of a lot easier when you get to a tree to chop it down if you've sharpened the axe first.

That's what mindfulness really is all about. Without a doubt, one of the most effective strategies for psychological flexibility is actually teaching mindfulness.

What mindfulness does is helps a person live fully in the present. This is important because those who have killed other people are often manifesting difficulty because of one of two things. They're living in the past, regretting it, reliving it, or re-experiencing it.

Or they're projecting into the future: "This means this," "I can't do this," "I can't do that," or "This is going to happen." They're paralyzed either by the past regrets or by the attempt to create meaning out of it, which is a "musterbatory" exercise, according to Ellis.

Mindfulness can be summarized by the words of the great Master Oogway. For those who don't know, Master Oogway was the turtle in *Kung Fu Panda*. He said, "Yesterday is history. Tomorrow is a mystery. Today is a gift, and that's why we call in the present."

Mindful living teaches a person to live in the present. When we have clients who have difficulty based on their previous experience of having taken another person's life, which is not something that the all-powerful therapist can absolve and resolve in one session.

But what can we do to help our clients experience a sense of stability, security, significance, and belonging? We can teach them to live fully in this moment.

Despite our past and no matter what happens in the future, we all have this moment—this one right here—this breath. Really, it's all any of us have.

Mindful living is about teaching your clients that no matter where they've been and no matter where they're going, in this moment, they have acceptance; in this moment, they're okay. As long as they are breathing, they are okay no matter what else is going on.

We teach our clients mindful living. We're actually going to guide you through a process of mindfulness. Mindfulness can be simply taught to a person by having them focus on their breath. We always have our breath with us from the first day of life until the end of life, so it makes a natural focal point to set aside the distress of yesterday or the worry about tomorrow.

For all clients, mindfulness really is key because they become active participators in life as opposed to reactive participants in life.

A lot of clients come in depressed because they're tired, and they're tired because they've been reacting, rather than responding.

They spend so much time in the past or so much time in the future. They live something over and over again, thinking, "What if?"

There's a quote that says, "Regret is our uncompromising idea that we can somehow change the past."

Or they spend so much time worrying about all the possible outcomes: "What will my life be like tomorrow, and next week?"

Mindfulness is a vital practice. It's been practiced not just in spiritual systems, but also in philosophical systems—the stoics, the Buddhists, the Hindus—throughout history as a strategy for living fully in the present.

Our goal with our clients is to bring them from where they've been to where they are now, which is even more important than getting them to where they think they want to go.

Purposeful Living: Turning Grief into a Crusade

One of the things that we identified as one of the praxeological needs is purposeful living. How can that be beneficial to a client?

First off, in our general course of clients, many of them say, "I feel like I have no purpose in life." Viktor Frankl covers this. Sometimes these events happen in our life, whether it's killing somebody or whatever else it may be, that may remove meaning or add some sort of negative or non-beneficial meaning.

A lot of times, instead of having clients achieve this overarching meaning or purpose to their life, we look to help them create a series of purposeful engagements. If there's grief, if there's guilt, if there's some sort of unresolved remnant of something going on, then we utilize that to create a crusade. The Adam Walsh Act—that requires the registration of sex offenders—is the perfect example. It saved the lives of a lot of people, even though the significance came from the grief of Adam's parents.

With the idea of the unresolved remnant, the idea of the part of your client that maybe that will never go away, what we can do is help them utilize that as something to go back to for inspiration. What type of purpose—what focus—can we use to create something?

Twenty years ago at Jack in the Box, through no fault of the restaurant, *E. coli* ended up in the beef and a bunch of kids died. That was one of the first national *E. coli* scares in the restaurant.

Jack in the Box restaurant, which could have lost everything, actually created a group called The Food Safety Council International. Unlike a lot of charitable organizations that companies create to cover up stuff, this one actually went about finding out what would contribute to safe food supply.

To this day, if you go into a Jack in the Box, it's one of the cleanest fast food restaurants there is. You'll always see the iced tea in a bag rather than simply in stainless steel. That's to make it easy for cleaning, because iced tea is actually the easiest place for *E. coli* and other bacteria to breed.

The corporate management took the death of those kids and turned it into something that has probably saved the lives of many people by investing resources into making their food safe, or at least as safe as you can make unhealthy fast food.

We had a client who had survivor's guilt. He wasn't drunk, but he was driving when he was in high school. He got in a car accident and a two of his friends were killed in that accident. For fifteen to twenty years he carried around this survivor's guilt.

In addition to all the other work we did, we looked for a crusade that he could either join or start. That way, he could take that unresolved remnant while we're working with it and turn it into a purpose. This goes back to creating meaning. We can create meaning that is beneficial both to the individual and to the world in general.

Problem-Solving Skills

Problem-solving skills are another area of need. With the old approach of Ericksonian therapists and Rogerian therapists, the client has within them all that they need. Richard always said that Rogerians who believe that haven't met his clients. A lot of clients really don't have problem-solving skills. They come from a background where they didn't have the psychological resources, or even the practical resources for problem solving, and they really don't know how to solve problems.

One of the most effective approaches to counseling is actually teaching. The first question in therapy is not, "So, what would you like to work on today?" The first question in therapy for me is always one that you ask yourself: "What does the client in front of me need to know in order to choose to do something different?" Maybe that's counters to cognitive errors, mindfulness, or problem-solving skills.

Richard worked at halfway house. One of the requirements of living there was that residents were either in job readiness training, or they were actively actually seeking gainful employment, or they had a job. They had to be doing one of those three things, or the fourth option was being kicked out.

A lot of the residents did not know how to get a job, how to write a resume, how to network, how to dress for an interview, how to bathe before an interview, or how to answer the questions.

For example, when they ask what are your three deficits in a job interview, these clients didn't know what to say. They would answer honestly, "I'm a messy pig who smells bad and is mean to people." What you should say is, "Well, I think that I'm trustworthy, and sometimes that becomes a deficit" or "I work too hard" or "I care too much."

But the residents literally didn't know this, so Richard had to teach them those things. You have to teach your client problem-solving skills. This book is designed to teach you the things that we need to teach our clients for them to experience wellness in light of the fact that they've killed other people.

Summing Up the Praxeological Approach

It's interesting how for the last ten thousand years up to the last hundred years we always understood human condition from religious experiences. Up until the last hundred, when psychology has replaced theology as the queen of social sciences, we always looked for a religious explanation—whether it was for a hurricane or an earthquake or war or whatever else.

Now, we draw on much more than just religion or just psychology. We pull in a little anthropology, a little psychology, a little sociology, a little biology to aid our clients with a praxeological approach.

POST-TRAUMATIC STRESS DISORDER IN THE DSM-5

As we've discussed elsewhere, not every client who has taken a life will be experiencing post-traumatic stress disorder (PTSD). Every person's reaction is different. That said, quite a few of the people who have taken a life do suffer from PTSD, so it's important that we are prepared to address the challenges that come with it. It's also important that we understand the diagnosis, as the American Psychiatric Association spells it out.

By the way, there was a lot of debate in the creation of the DSM-5 around the question of whether it should be called PTS or PTSD. The DSM-5 continues to use the "Disorder" rather than just "Post-Traumatic Stress"—dropping the "disorder". That was really a bone of contention in the DSM-5 because some therapists argue that stress is simply a realistic reaction to experiencing traumatic events. While the DSM-5 kept the longer term, it can be useful to view your clients through that normalizing frame: they are simply normal people reacting normally to abnormal circumstances.

Before we get into the material related to treatment methods and strategies for impacting post-traumatic stress disorder, we want to talk about some of the significant changes in the DSM-5. The criteria have been changed to some extent, creating a broader base for whom the diagnosis of post-traumatic stress disorder is available.

One of the significant changes is that Criterion C has actually been broken down into two parts: Criteria C and D. By the way, if you're wondering where you can look at the new diagnostic criteria for the DSM-5, you can always go to www.dsm5.org and look at the American Psychiatric Association's web page.

One of the most important aspects of providing the correct intervention with clients is actually providing a correct diagnosis. Post-traumatic stress disorder, over the past couple of decades, has become to some extent a psychofad. It appears that at various times in our profession we latch on to one diagnosis as the catchall for clients who are having difficulty.

For a while it was bipolar disorder that was the popular diagnosis. For a while it was post-traumatic stress disorder. For a while it seemed like every kid had oppositional-defiant disorder. It seems at various times diagnoses are popularized and over-extended so that any client who experiences stress or difficulty in life receives a particular diagnosis. If our client says that they have difficulties or problems as a result of a previous experience in life, we've tended to simply diagnose that as post-traumatic stress disorder.

One of the best things about the DSM is it has always been very thorough, not in all areas, but particularly as it deals with post-traumatic stress disorder. There are very specific criteria that must be met for a person to receive a diagnosis of post-traumatic stress disorder. This is very important because when we diagnose somebody without an awareness of the diagnostic criteria, we tend to over-diagnose and that tends to lead to over-treatment, both in terms of medication and intensity of psychotherapy.

Also, if we look at the other conditions that a person may experience related to disaster syndrome or acute stress disorder or other diagnoses that are available to us, we can truly meet our clients' needs by being accurate. The most effective intervention really is accurate assessment. The DSM-5 makes some significant changes from the DSM-IV in post-traumatic stress disorder.

So before we get into the material looking at evidence-based treatment and the methods of working with these folks, let's take a few minutes to familiarize you with the criteria from the DSM-5.

First of all, these criteria apply only to adults, adolescents, and children older than six. There is a preschool subtype for children younger than age six in the DSM-5. This is the first significant change, essentially a preschool PTSD diagnosis. We are not experts in treating the preschool child. We work primarily with adults and adolescents. Because this is an area that is not our expertise, it's a very significant and important change for us as well as for those who do work with preschool aged children. We're not going to discuss the criteria and interventions for the preschool PTSD. But if you work with that population, certainly there are some significant changes that you should be aware of.

Here are the criteria that must be met. There are four diagnostic groupings:

> ***Criterion A:*** *There has to be an exposure to an actual or threatened (a) death (b) serious injury (c) sexual violation in at least one or more of the following ways:*
>
> 1. *Directly experiencing the traumatic event.*
> 2. *Witnessing in person the traumatic events as they occurred to others.*

Let me give an example from September 11, 2001. We all watched on TV the horror of the World Trade Center buildings coming down in New York City. Most of us watched on television as people fell from the upper floors of the World Trade Center, or possibly leapt because it was really their only escape and they knew that they were dying. In fact, there was a famous picture called "Falling Man" that actually won a Pulitzer journalism award. It was a devastating day.

Many of us watched that on television. Even though we may have had very intense emotional responses to it, the diagnosis of post-traumatic stress disorder isn't made because we saw something on television. It can only be made when we are actually witnessing in person the traumatic events as they occur to others. There is no diagnosis of vicarious post-traumatic stress disorder.

> 3. *Learning that the traumatic event occurred to close family members or a close friend. Cases of actual or threatened death must be violent or accidental, not simply the result of illness, which can also be traumatic for a family member.*
> 4. *Experiencing repeated or extreme exposure to aversive details of the traumatic event.*

Item #4 refers to first responders collecting human remains, police officers repeatedly exposed to details of child abuse, that sort of thing. This does not apply to exposure through electronic media, television, movies, or pictures, unless the exposure is work- related.

The DSM-5 committee has been very careful to avoid an expanded diagnosis of vicarious PTSD. Seeing these events unfold on live TV or something like that are not considered as the diagnostic criteria for post-traumatic stress disorder, even though they may be distressing.

When a person has experienced the actual event in one or more of those ways, then we can look at criterion B.

> ***Criterion B:*** *The presence of one or more specific intrusive symptoms associated with the traumatic event.*

The keyword here is "intrusive symptoms". We're going to spend a lot of time talking about how we stop the intrusion of these thoughts that really torment those with post-traumatic stress disorder.

There has to be presence of one or more of the intrusive symptoms beginning after the traumatic event has occurred. In other words, there are some people who had intrusive symptoms prior to events and events may exacerbate those. The diagnostic criteria require that these are new intrusive symptoms in order for a diagnosis of PTSD to be made; otherwise we may be dealing with somebody with a generalized or other form of anxiety disorder. Here are those five intrusive symptoms:

1. *Spontaneous or cued recurrent, involuntary and intrusive distressing memories of traumatic events. Note: In children, play may occur in which themes or aspects of the traumatic event are expressed.*

2. *Recurrent, distressing dreams in which the content or affect of the dream is related to the event. Note: In children, there may be frightening dreams without recognizable content.*

For children, there may be frightening dreams without recognizable content because they're not at that cognitive developmental stage of the subconscious mind where it would be necessarily attributed to the event. In the adult, we're looking for dreams and affective aspects of those dreams that the dreamer (the client) directly relates to the traumatic event they experience, sometimes called nighttime terrors.

3. *Dissociative reactions (flashback) in which the individual feels or acts as if the traumatic event is recurring. Such reactions may occur on a continuum with the most extreme expression being a complete loss*

of awareness of the present surroundings. Note: In young children, trauma-specific reenactment may occur.

Essentially the term we use in hypnosis is a revivification of the experience. They're not simply recalling something from the past, but they're actually reliving that experience from the past. That is on the continuum of flashbacks or dissociative reactions, the most extreme noted in the DSM-5.

4. *Intense or prolonged psychological distress at exposure to internal or external cues that either symbolize or resemble an aspect of a traumatic event.*

This is, using hypnotic language, the concept of anchoring. We anchor our emotions and experiences in life to a variety of environmental cues. Almost everybody can relate to this: Have you ever been driving down the road and you're just doing whatever it is when you drive down the road and you're not even paying attention to the radio, but suddenly a song comes up and you haven't heard the song in five, ten, fifteen, or twenty years but as soon as that song comes on the radio, instantly you are jolted out of your automatic driving behavior and you become aware of not only the song but an emotion associated with it and maybe even a prior life event?

Musicians write music that is designed to evoke emotion. This is the goal of many musicians. They sell more when there's an emotional response. Most of us can relate to simply going about the task of the day and that song instantly changing our mood. It makes us happy or it brings us into a state of depression or it reminds us of a prior life experience.

This is really a normal experience that everybody has in life related to certain environmental and awareness cues that are in our everyday life. It becomes diagnostic for post-traumatic stress disorder when opening a door becomes an emotional cue to revivify/flashback to a prior experience, or when a loud noise, an unexpected experience, a news report, or the simple mundane things in life bring a person back specifically to traumatic prior events.

> 5. *A marked physiological reaction to reminders of traumatic events.*

One of the things we need to recognize in the history of the DSM-IV an DSM-5, even back to the DSM-III, although the DSM-5 puts post-traumatic stress disorder in its own section of stress-related disorders, in the past it was included in the anxiety disorder section.

Anxiety disorders and anxiety are particularly physical. Many of our clients with post-traumatic stress disorder not only have emotional and cognitive awareness of prior events and experiences, but they have a physical response to the traumas that they have experienced before. They're somatic in their manifestation of the psychological distress that they experience.

The keyword is marked. We're looking for marked physical reactions to the reminders of traumatic events: everything ranging from shakiness to sweatiness to palpitations to the feeling of butterflies in the stomach, or really any of the other physiological symptoms that we may see in the other sections of the DSM-IV where they showed the panic related to anxiety disorder.

For many of the post-traumatic stress disorder clients that we've worked with over the years, it is these physiological responses that are actually the most distressing to them. They begin to fear that they're having a heart attack, or they begin to fear that they're dying. They begin to feel those physiological manifestations and that often becomes the most difficult thing for them.

As psychotherapists, our attention is often focused on the emotional aspects of a problem, but these physiological aspects can be one of the most distressing of symptoms.

The major change in the DSM-5 was really taking the C criterion from the DSM-IV and creating a C and D.

> ***Criterion C:*** *Persistent avoidance of stimuli associated with the traumatic event beginning after the traumatic event occurred as evidenced by efforts to do one or more of the following.*

What we have is the persistent intrusion of experiences or the client going to extremes to avoid those persistent intrusions. Here are two of the ways people might make that effort:

> 1. *Distressing memories, thoughts, or feelings that are closely associated with the traumatic event are avoided at all cost.*

For example, they never open that bedroom window again or they never go back to that intersection again or they refuse to watch TV ever again or they won't talk to people ever again. They'll do anything to avoid the distressing memory, or distressing thought, or distressing feeling.

> 2. *Avoidance of external reminders: people, places, conversations, activities, situations that arouse distressing memories, thoughts, or feelings that are closely associated with the traumatic event.*

> ***Criterion D:*** *Negative alterations in cognitions and mood associated with the traumatic events beginning or worsening after the event occurred as evidenced by two or more of the following:*

(It's sort of subtle, but *after the event occurred* is really important. There are people with anxiety and stress-related disorders and depressive features who sometimes manifest these things prior to the onset of a trauma. For a diagnosis of PTSD to be made, there must be a unique response to the trauma discussed in Criterion A, or else a different diagnosis is made.)

1. *The inability to remember an important aspect of a traumatic event.*
2. *Persistent and exaggerated negative beliefs or expectations about oneself or the world.*

Some examples include:

"I'm bad."

"No one can be trusted."

"The world is completely dangerous."

"I've lost my soul forever."

"My whole nervous system is permanently ruined."

Often these beliefs are all-or-nothing thoughts.

3. *Persistent distorted blame of self or others about the cause or consequence of the traumatic event.*

It could be related to survivor's guilt to some extent.

4. *Persistent negative emotional states: fear, horror, anger, guilt, shame.*

Persistent is the keyword. We all have some negative emotional states at one point or another. We're looking for persistence in them.

5. *A markedly diminished interest or participation in significant activities.*

For example, "Before the trauma, I loved bowling. Now I won't bowl. I find no joy or pleasure in it."

6. *Feelings of detachment or estrangement from others.*

This is an involuntary shift in perceptual position where they can no longer see or experience their life as them, but see it as an outsider in the detachment from those who are most important to them.

7. A persistent inability to experience positive emotions.

We have the presence of those persistent negative emotions coupled with a persistent inability to experience positive emotions: unable to have loving feelings, a sense of psychic numbing, the inability to feel happy or to smile or to feel a sense of even relief, safety, or security.

Criterion E: *Marked alterations in arousal reactivity associated with the traumatic event.*

When there is a cue, a remembrance, a subconscious or conscious awareness, the alterations in arousal reactivity beginning or worsening after the traumatic event as evidenced by at least two or more of the following:

1. *Irritable or aggressive behavior.*
2. *Reckless or self-destructive behavior.*
3. *Hypervigilance.*
4. *Exaggerated startle response.*
5. *Problems with concentration.*
6. *Sleep disturbances (difficulty falling asleep or difficulty remaining asleep or restless sleep, waking up too early, etc.)*

In the clients we've worked with over the years, sleep disturbances seem to be among the most impairing symptoms. Most people only function as well during the day as they slept the evening before. Our clients who have difficulty with sleep as the result of the intrusiveness or the alterations of arousal and reactivity related to dreams and sleep experience a tremendous amount of difficulty in relation to PTSD.

Again, for a diagnosis to be made, it has to appear after the traumatic event. For example, some people have a heightened startle response. If you were just to say, "Boo!" they would tend to jump.

This would not be diagnostic. You would have to look for one of two of the other criteria because that was already present in their life prior to any difficult experience.

Then of course there are a couple of other things that involve time duration and rule-outs that the DSM-5 gives us.

> ***Criterion F:*** *The duration of the disturbance (Criterion B, C, D, and E) is more than one month.*

In other words, if you experience a car wreck, it's normal to be shaken for days or even weeks. It's not PTSD unless you are still affected by it more than a month later.

Richard relates:

> *I actually did have a car accident several years ago. I was driving down the street, on my street where I live, and a lady just bought a brand new car. I feel bad for her. It was her first day. She had it for two hours. This tells you how long ago it was: she was trying to figure out how to work the cassette deck, and she didn't see the stop sign. She went through the stop sign and T-boned me.*

> *Both cars spun around. Hers hit a tree. I saw that I was okay, so I ran out to get her. She was okay. Both of our cars were totaled, and both of us were okay. The police came and did the accident investigation. I felt bad for her. They towed off the cars, and I went home.*

> *Over the next couple days, it was interesting. I kept having dreams of going through that intersection, but instead of me being hit by a car, I would drive over the neighborhood kids. My dreams were really weird. I kept dreaming that the neighborhood kids were two-dimensional popups from the street. It would wake me up.*

> *This continued and I had other symptoms related to this experience. I would be driving down the road and dodge*

imaginary cars that weren't there. This all went on for a week or two, maybe even three, and those symptoms all disappeared. In fact, I haven't thought about them until I started talking about this and it came back to me.

What's important is it's normal to experience these symptoms after a traumatic event. The diagnosis can only be made when these symptoms persist for more than one month. That's really important. Nobody on September 21, 2001, in New York City, no matter where they were on September 11, could be diagnosed with PTSD. The reason why is that at least thirty days must have lapsed before a diagnosis could be made—because it is normal for us to experience these things in the short term.

Some experts talk about four months. We can bring it down to the first four months is an acute stress phase, and then the four- to eight-month period is the acute PTSD phase, and then eight months or longer could be viewed as the chronic phase where the symptoms continue. We do see this as a continuum.

> ***Criterion G:*** *The disturbance has to cause clinically significant distress or impairment in social, occupational, or other important areas of functioning.*

This may sound obvious, but sometimes people just have strange responses. If it's not causing impairment, if it's not distressing to them or if it's only distressing to us or other family members—sometimes the behavior of others just irritates us—that's not PTSD. That's somebody in the family not allowing a person to experience life the way they want to experience life.

It has to cause clinically significant distress or impairment: not going to work, not getting out of the house, not getting up and taking a shower during the day, not eating, not sleeping, not taking care of oneself.

> ***Criterion H:*** *The disturbance is not attributed to the direct physiological effects of a substance.*

Examples include medication, drugs, alcohol, or another medical condition like a brain injury, a stroke, or other types of situations we have.

We then have in the DSM-5 the ability to give specifiers. We can specify if it is with delayed expression—if the diagnostic threshold is not exceeded until at least six months after the event. This is something we see. They don't immediately go into PTSD on day 31. They seem to hold it together.

Maybe there's even a conscious or subconscious activation of these symptoms so that the onset is literally a delayed expression. They don't emerge meeting the criteria until at least six months after the event. That is a specifier we can list.

The DSM-5 also gives us the post-traumatic stress disorder in preschool children, which we will let you review at DSM5.org rather than covering it here since the focus is not on children under age six. Many of the ideas we're going to talk about would actually be useful with that age group, but again that's not our particular area of expertise. We'll be focusing on children, adolescents, and adults, but not the preschool population or the preschool subtype.

Then we have another subtype that is available to us in the DSM-5, and that is the post-traumatic stress disorder with prominent dissociative symptoms. These symptoms are depersonalization and derealization.

In this experience, the person meets the diagnostic criteria for PTSD. In addition to that, the experiences persist or reoccur symptoms of either:

> 1.   *Depersonalization: An experience of being detached from, or as if one is an outside observer of, one's*

> *mental process or their body, feeling as if they're in a dream, a sense of unreality of self or body or of time distortion and time moving slowly or quickly.*
>
> 2.   *Derealization: An experience of unreality of one's surroundings; the world around the person seems unreal, dreamlike, distant, or distorted.*

The symptoms are not due to the results of a substance: cannabis, alcohol, benzodiazepine, sedative hypnotic, other prescription or nonprescription medication, or a health condition.

For those working with preschool children: note that the dissociative and preschool subtypes are not necessarily mutually exclusive. If you work with the preschool population, a dissociative and preschool PTSD subtype diagnosis can actually be made simultaneously.

One of the other significant changes in the DSM-5 is it's really reliant on measures of severity. Using the Global Assessment of Functioning that we were familiar with in the DSM-IV, we gave a GAF score between 0-100. The DSM-5 looks at it entirely different. They've done away with the multiaxial system; the DSM-5 asks us to really assess the severity of client condition within each diagnostic category.

The DSM-5 uses the National Stressful Events Survey of PTSD Short Scale (the NSESSS) from the National Institute of Health. You can find this on DSM5.org where you can go to the diagnostic criteria for post-traumatic stress disorder and click on the severity tab.

It's a self-report that asks the client to measure nine areas of the severity of their condition based on those prior criteria. These types of tools can be really useful for the clinician to conceptualize progress and recovery, severity of condition, and the acuity of client condition. This is really important.

Of course, not every client who has killed is the same, and some of them will not suffer from PTSD. That's why it's important to understand the diagnostic criteria and refrain from jumping to conclusions.

SUICIDE RISK

We need to discuss suicide and suicide risk. The epidemiological studies related to post-traumatic stress disorder indicate that compared to people with any of the other psychiatric diagnoses in the DSM-5, those with a diagnosis of post-traumatic stress disorder are at an exponentially greater risk of suicide.

In assessing suicide risk in those who have PTSD, the research points out that there are really four things we're looking for:

1. Duration of PTSD Symptoms
2. Alcohol and Cannabis Use
3. History of Prior Abuse
4. Presence of Depression

First, we're looking for a duration that's chronic (more than one year of symptoms). One of the first questions we ask as we measure severity is, "How long has this been going on for you?" If it's been going on for more than one year, the epidemiological studies show this person is at an elevated risk for suicide.

The second thing we're looking for is: are they a pot smoker or alcohol user? These are the two drugs associated with post-traumatic stress disorder self-medicating, which increases the risks for suicidal expression and suicidal action.

The third thing we're looking for is a history of prior abuse. In the field of psychotherapy, therapists often still rely on Freud's idea that a problem could develop today because of prior experiences.

In general, we don't believe that we are tied today to our prior experiences. But in cases of PTSD, we often have a person who had unresolved childhood PTSD that wasn't effectively treated. Because the resolution was never dealt with following physical and sexual abuse, clients double down on their symptoms and their inability to cope as an adult when they are re-traumatized. What this does is exacerbate the situation, intensity, severity, and coping strategies, and we see this as an issue.

The fourth thing we're looking for as we measure severity of condition is whether there is significant depression coupled with the PTSD. Going beyond symptoms of anxiety, intrusive and distressing symptoms, do we see clinical depression?

Here's the interesting thing about the DSM-5. Because we don't have a multiaxial system anymore, we simply can have multiple diagnoses. We can have PTSD and a diagnosis of major depression coupled with other psychiatric diagnoses. When we see major depression coupled with post-traumatic stress disorder, we have a person who is exponentially at greater risk for suicide.

Let's spend some time talking about some specific issues related to suicidal ideation. This is a very important area to address.

Because the PTSD client is at an exponentially greater risk for suicide, and because those who have taken a life may experience PTSD, we want to make sure that we cover some of the basic indicators we need to look for.

The first is from a demographic perspective. Who is at greatest risk for suicide? Ask this questions to mental health professionals, and they'll say its teenagers or college-aged kids. Actually, with each year of life, we increase suicide risk, which is why when we're dealing with PTSD in the Vietnam veterans who are in their 60s, 70s, and 80s at this point, we're really looking at elevated suicide risk, especially if depression, alcohol addiction, and untreated PTSD have been present.

The older a person is, the more likely they are to attempt and succeed at suicide. Men, interestingly enough, are twice as likely to succeed at suicide than women. But women are twice as likely to attempt suicide. The reason why is, men tend to choose more lethal methods. Men choose hanging and gunshots. Women choose cutting and overdosing. Gunshots and hanging are more lethal so it results in more deaths, even though females actually have more suicide attempts.

By the way, never underestimate the importance of suicide attempts, even if the attempt was not actually intended to cause death, because more people accidentally die trying to kill themselves than actually die because they genuinely intended to kill themselves.

There are cultural and racial differences in the prevalence of suicide. Whites are at greatest risk followed by Native Americans, followed by African-Americans, and then followed by Hispanics.

The unmarried person is more likely to both succeed and attempt suicide than the unmarried person. There is an elevation with those who self-identify as being homosexual.

Of course we're looking for family history of suicide or a close friend who's committed suicide. This is often, but not necessarily, hereditary. There could be some biological aspects, but when they've seen somebody else succeed at suicide—either someone close to them or someone famous—they actually receive the message, "Wow, that worked." So they're more likely to both attempt and succeed at suicide. This is actually called the "Werther Effect." The diagnosis of PTSD exponentially increases the risk.

All PTSD clients should be assessed on a regular basis for suicidal ideation. When we're doing that, we should be asking for a couple of things. Do they have thoughts of suicide? It's not abnormal for people to think about suicide, especially if it happens to be a topic in the news. There was recently an executive who jumped from a bridge, and it became a national story. People think about it.

What we want to know though is how intrusive those thoughts are. How frequent are those thoughts? What's the quality of those thoughts?

Then we want to know if they have a plan: "I think about. I don't know how I would do it" versus "I think about, yeah. I have a gun, and that's how I would do it."

The next step is coupling that plan with a contingency: "I would implement the plan predicated on this happening." In other words, "If I can't stop being depressed, then I'll do it," or "If I get one more letter from the IRS, then I'll do it," or "If my wife leaves me, then I'll do it," or "If they fire me from my job, then I'll do it."

Is there a plan coupled with a contingency? A point where they would move to the next level of suicidal ideation? Keep a watchful eye.

Then we're looking for a prior attempt. Does the person have a history of prior suicide attempts? The best indicator for future behavior is past behavior. Each suicide attempt often becomes more lethal and more likely to succeed than the last. Of course how recent that previous suicide attempt is exponentially increases the risk of another suicide attempt.

If we have a previous suicide attempt, by the way, we have to ask the question: Did the client believe it would cause death? There are a lot of people who have attempted suicide in the past knowing that the method wasn't particularly lethal and they might not die. Then there are people who survived in spite of the suicide attempt.

This happens with a lot of adolescents. They believe if they take fourteen Tylenol and seventeen Vitamin B it's going to kill them. So they do and they end up in ICU with liver damage, but they don't end up dying from it. However, did they believe it would kill them? That's one of the things we want to assess in the prior attempts.

What about motivation? Do they have a motivation to die? Do they have a motivation to live? What are their motivation levels? These are the types of things we're looking for in our assessment of suicidal ideation: prior suicide attempts, the demographics, and the history.

We could easily write a whole book focusing on suicidal ideation. On www.fastceus.com we actually have an audio course on that. But it is important if you're dealing with the PTSD diagnosed client, or anyone who has taken a life, to be aware of the indicators of suicidal ideation and the risk factors that are present and have knowledge and training in that area because PTSD clients are, of all the psychiatric diagnoses we work with, at greatest risk for taking their own life.

Application

Introduction to Interventions: Using Evidence-Based Strategies

As we share with you intervention ideas and strategies, we're going to draw from the research. It is vital to look at what the research tells us is most effective to our work with clients.

Edna Foa is a professor and editor of a book titled *Effective Treatment for PTSD*. The second edition came out in 2010. It has a lot of really useful information. As a country, and even in the world of psychology and counseling, we're in a post-911 era. Our understanding of PTSD has increased as ten years-plus of war have certainly provided us with many more case studies and individuals who have been traumatized by the experiences they have. Within the last ten years, we have also increased awareness of the relationship between childhood sexual abuse and post-traumatic stress disorder.

Foa talks about those treatment protocols, which have demonstrated efficacy. As we go through the various processes of helping people make change, these are the things we're going to share. There are a lot of things in the book that we're not necessarily going to touch on, and we're going to add a few things, but it's really important to look at the research—not simply tradition or the approach that we feel would be best with our client or the approach that would be best for us.

The research shows us that there are a couple of things that really are highly effective with post-traumatic stress disorder. The first on the list is cognitive behavioral therapy. The great thing about cognitive behavioral therapy is we can integrate CBT into other modalities of treatment.

There are advances in pharmacotherapy which can actually assist some of our clients who are at an acute phase—characterized by suicidal ideation, disorganized thinking, dissociative states—to be able to move to a point of wellness where we can teach long-term strategies for change. No psychotropic has ever healed somebody and made them well, but many psychotropics have helped stabilize people, allowing them to avoid catastrophe and crisis so they can move them to a point of developing wellness.

One of the other outcome-based treatments that has gained a lot of attention both from the military and elsewhere is Eye Movement and Desensitization Therapy (EMDR), which some people view as a form of hypnotherapy, though its advocates loudly deny that idea.

We were very happy to see Edna Foa include both in her first and second edition an entire chapter on the efficacy of hypnotherapy as a strategy for dealing with post-traumatic stress disorder. Your authors are both certified clinical hypnotherapists. We do a lot of training people on clinical hypnotherapy. Hypnotherapy is one of those great tools for helping a person to take physical control over the difficulties that they experience.

Some hypnotic techniques involve a formal "trance" or visualization experience. Others, like the Submodality Shifting exercise we'll demonstrate, are more interactive and conversational.

Emotional Freedom Technique (EFT), sometimes called "tapping," is another fascinating area. It's been to some extent controversial in the field of psychotherapy, mostly because of disagreement over how it works. However, if you look at efficacy of EFT in the research, you'll see mountains of evidence supporting its use with a wide variety of clients. We'll devote a chapter to teaching some EFT techniques.

As we talk about these interventions, this isn't a matter of "do this first, then do this, then do this." Each person is going to be entirely different. There is no set protocol, but rather a toolbox full of effective interventions for you to use as you see fit.

USING RAPPORT: THE GENTLE APPROACH

Rapport in therapy is probably the number one indicator of the successful intervention of the therapist. First understanding and having the client feel understood about their model in this case, whether it's with a soldier or a criminal, create rapport. If you project your model onto them, they will feel incongruent—either thinking they don't agree with you or becoming confused about how they feel.

How do you establish rapport with someone who has taken a life?

First off, take a gentle approach towards the client. As a therapist, you probably engage in this anyway. You know to allow the client to be right where they are at the time they are.

This can be a particular challenge, especially in cases involving PTSD. These types of clients have typically closed themselves off, experiencing derealization and dissociative symptoms. When your clients don't see themselves as being a part of something, it can really be difficult to bring yourself in rapport with those folks.

Another challenge with rapport is that once we have it established, we become an authority figure. We become trusted. Maybe the client is just processing some challenging feelings at the time, but they may not have a full-blown case of PTSD in the way that it's defined in the DSM-5. Once we have established rapport with them and they trust us, if we say, "I think you might have PTSD" or something similar, then we may actually be giving them the suggestion to develop PTSD.

We're not sure exactly why that can happen in certain people. We do know that people with a higher level of neuropeptide Y are more resistant to PTSD. The military is aware of this as they deal with Special Forces and special ops. They did studies to find out why people in the special operations community had a much lower incidence of PTSD even though they were the ones who were more often than not engaged in combat.

What they found was that Special Forces operatives had higher levels of neuropeptide Y. In fact, they could almost determine who would make it through the selection course of almost any service and any special operations force. They could tell who would make it through, from a psychological perspective, by the levels of neuropeptide Y, because of the ability to handle stress. They know that neuropeptide Y is that buffer to stress.

This is an important thing. There are many ideas as to why people develop PTSD. We have to recognize that we are a combination of our biological factors, our psychological factors, learnings, copings, our spiritual factors of how well we are meeting our deepest needs, and the social resources and factors around us and to recognize why one person who experiences it.

Not every firefighter and police officer in New York City on September 11th developed PTSD. Not everybody in the building did who escaped. But some did go on to develop PTSD. What is the difference?

This gets a little controversial. When we look at the suicide rate amongst the active duty military and veterans, we see that right now it's currently over twenty per day, which is high obviously—22% higher than non-veteran adults.

Most civilians think, "They've been in combat and seen these horrible things, and that's why they commit suicide."

But the reality of the situation is many of them have not been in combat. Studies have shown that about 45% of the PTSD cases involve returning veterans who saw no combat.

In 2011, a study of 112 guardsmen who had committed suicide showed that half of them had never even deployed.

That is an example of rapport and social contagion leading to PTSD and suicide. Asking the questions, "Why do so many veterans have PTSD? Why are so many veterans committing suicide?" offers essentially hypnotic suggestion that PTSD and suicide are to be expected. This is why you have to be so careful about what you say to your clients, especially when you have established rapport.

Look at all the messages that are in the media now about broken veterans, about PTSD, about the difficulties of returning home. Returning home could be difficult. You're going from one world to another and trying to integrate those two, and a lot of times it's the cultural integration stress that starts creating the isolation more than what happened over there.

Coming home can be challenging: Trying to reintegrate into your family, trying to reintegrate into society. You leave and your kid can't talk, and then you come home and your kid is telling you to move out of his chair. All of the sudden, your world is entirely different.

Think of a veteran who maybe does not have a college degree and goes over there and spends maybe four years in the military, is a sergeant or a staff sergeant in the army in whatever branch of service, but has leadership responsibilities, has led troops in combat, or at least managed troops in daily activities.

Then they come back and can't get a job because they don't have a degree. The civilian world doesn't recognize their leadership experience, so they take a step down in their own significance and their own certainty.

So when we see the problems that could have a cause other than trauma, we suppose it is veteran PTSD, when it could be any number of problems involved with reintegration.

Our culture and its media are out of balance. We talk about the wounded veteran and the need to be compassionate. All of that is true, but we don't say soldiers also return with valor, confidence, and pride.

Almost every big story now may be a hero story, but it's a hero story from the angle of the broken veteran who's doing okay—not from somebody who just came back and readjusted and got on with their life. That's not a newsworthy story. We forget that psychological resilience is actually the norm, not the exception.

That's why it's necessary to build rapport and use the gentle approach—a nonjudgmental approach that goes both ways: not judging the soldier as weak, but also not just jumping in and saying, "I know you're going through a really hard time now," because that's feeding into what the rest of society is giving them. If you're dealing with veterans, that may cause your clients to question their own resilience.

It goes back to some of the criticisms of critical incident stress management. For years, people have been taught that if you have somebody who has experienced trauma, you need to do critical incident stress debriefing. You need to get them talking about it, get them to share it, get it out on the table. The research shows that's actually contraindicated, and with many folks, it is actually harmful.

Rapport is best not when you tell your clients what they need to be investing in therapy, but when the clients decide in therapy what is most important to them. People may not present with a diagnosis of PTSD. If you're a marriage and family therapist, like Richard, you may see people coming in because of money trouble and marital problems.

But then we may see the presenting problem—marriage counseling—is not the actual problem, which in this case is PTSD. But you have to allow the client to set that agenda in therapy.

When you've worked with thousands of people in therapy, you may know your client has a particular issue. They don't see it as their issue yet, but they're going to in three or four months of therapy because that's what happens in therapy. So why don't you just get it out on the table now?

While it's tempting to try to cut to the chase, truth is your clients have to come to the conclusion themselves a lot of times. The role of a therapist is, in a way, an influencer role. Whether you're a therapist or a salesman or any other kind of influencer, it's always far more persuasive when clients reach the conclusion on their own.

If they haven't gotten to that point yet and they're unwilling to accept it, then you're going to meet resistance. The more often you go at it, then the more resistance they put up.

So if a point in time comes when they actually realize that you were right, they may not even admit it because now they've built up so much resistance and have identified so much of that resistance that they won't let it go.

The flipside of that is if you do have a veteran in particular—and even non-veterans right now, because it's such a hot topic—if they come in having self-diagnosed and they say, "I have PTSD," it's okay to offer them an alternative:

"How do you know you have PTSD?" you can ask.

"Because I have this symptom and that symptom."

You can say, "Well, you're right. You may have PTSD, but it might just be this and this." Give them an option other than PTSD.

What are some basic strategies for building rapport? Most therapists are really pretty comfortable with a lot of different types of people with different backgrounds and different experiences. But sometimes we do encounter clients who, for some reason, we either don't feel a connection to, or around whom we may feel intimidated by their experience or other things. What are some basic strategies for building rapport on a very simple level?

One is to maintain your frame as the therapist. As a health care provider, you have to guard against being overly helpful or overly empathetic because that may not be what they need at that time. Be friendly to your clients, but don't be their friend. Give them advice and wisdom, but don't try to be their mother. Stay in the role of therapist. They'll test us to see if we'll transgress that role and become their friend or become their enemy. If we can listen to anything without raising our eyebrow, we pass the test.

Rapport is often misunderstood. It's multifaceted, and a lot of people think that rapport is simply your client liking you. But in the role of an influencer, rapport goes so much deeper. David did three different boot camps, three different basic trainings: the Marine Corps, the Navy, and the Army. Boot camp trainees are not friends with the drill instructors or drill sergeants. The drill sergeants are not the recruits' buddies.

But probably three or four weeks into training, if the recruits thought the instructors were disappointed in them, the recruits tried harder. You could say that's Stockholm syndrome or anything else, but isn't that deep rapport right there? It wasn't that the instructors were their friends, but the recruits knew that the instructors had the recruits' best interests at heart.

That's important for your clients to know. They need to know that you have their best interest at heart, that you are their advocate, even though your are not their friend, even though you are not their mother, even though your are not their lover, spouse, or any other role that sometimes occasionally we see confusion on.

From a rapport-building perspective, one great idea is questioning. It goes back to an old story about a guy who gets invited to a millionaire's house and he wants to impress him. So what does he do? Instead of telling the millionaire how great he is, he simply spends the whole night long asking the millionaire questions about himself. At the end of the evening, the millionaire basically says, "Wow, you're the greatest conversationalist ever." The millionaire knows nothing about him but hires him for a grand task anyway.

Here's your interview tip. When you go see the interviewer, they're going to start asking questions about you. You start asking questions about them. "I see you have a dragon in your office. Have you been to Asia before?" That's going to build rapport. The interviewer will think, "Somebody was finally interested in me."

Most therapists are good talkers, so it's really easy to be in that teacher role with the clients and tell them what they need to know. Really pay attention to that, so that you can ask what your clients need and simply let them explore their own solutions in the questioning process that you guide them through.

To sum it up, the gentle approach involves setting a framework in which your clients can reach their own conclusions. It involves maintaining your distance so that you don't force your preconceptions onto your clients, but also a benevolence that allows the clients enough safety to discover not only their own problems, but also their own solutions.

CONTEXTUAL PSYCHOLOGY

There are a number of different intervention techniques to use with those who have killed others (whether they have PTSD or not): clinical hypnotherapy, EFT, and cognitive-behavioral therapy, to name a few. Clinical hypnotherapy is really a tremendous tool for dealing with panic, anxiety, and many of the symptoms we see related to PTSD.

However, regardless of the specific technique used, we approach clients from a perspective of contextual psychology. Contextual psychology is a set of evidence-based or outcome-based treatment protocols that utilize what psychological researchers have shown us to be the most effective methods of helping people make change.

Contextual psychology includes the work of John Kabat-Zinn at the University of Massachusetts on Mindfulness-based Stress Reduction, Marsha Linehan and her work in Dialectical Behavioral Therapy, Solution-focused Brief Therapy from Steve de Shazer and Insoo Kim Berg, Steven Hayes at the University of Nevada and his Acceptance and Commitment Therapy.

Just like the presuppositions about those who have killed other people, there are certain presuppositions that we are going to operate from as we teach you some specific interventions. The presuppositions are drawn from contextual psychology:

1. We cannot avoid pain; we can only mitigate our suffering.

2. It is often the coping strategies that we employ that make us suffer.
3. Fusion with emotions creates paralysis.
4. It is the meaning we give thoughts that leads to distress.

The first presupposition is that we can't avoid pain. Life is painful. To try to help people avoid pain is really a futile effort. What we *can* do is help a person mitigate their suffering, even though we can't avoid pain.

The second thing is it's often the coping strategy that we employ that makes us suffer. Unfortunately, therapy often actually reiterates the ineffective coping strategy and exacerbates the suffering.

Psychologist Edna Foa has done a lot of research with others on evidence-based treatment protocols for post-traumatic stress reduction. For years, therapists thought that immediately talking about an event immediately after it happened was the best way to debrief a person and avoid post-traumatic stress disorder. What the research shows is that strategy actually exacerbates the situation. It revivifies the experience.

Yet the opposite choice—trying not to think about the problem—is no more effective. That's the coping strategies that our clients most often employ, yet it can cause them suffering. For example, people will say, "I don't want to think about that traumatic event. I don't want to think about that experience. I want to put it out of my mind." But in order to think about putting it out of your mind in order to put it out of your mind, you have to think about it, so you'll know what to put out of your mind.

To illustrate this, as you read this paragraph, think about anything you want to, except a yellow jeep. Think about anything you want to at this time, except a yellow jeep. Do not let yourself think about a yellow jeep. Stop thinking about a yellow jeep and think about something else. The harder you try not to think of a yellow jeep, the more you start to see yellow jeeps everywhere.

Many traditional psychotherapy approaches, including suppressive strategies, are contraindicated with many of our clients.

The third presupposition of contextual psychology is it's the fusion with emotions that creates paralysis—and really suffering too. As opposed to feeling our emotions—"I feel anger" or "I feel remorse"—we become our emotions—"I am angry" or "I am remorseful." When we are fused with our emotions, they can overwhelm us.

So in contextual hypnotherapy, we help a person create an observational perceptual position, an observational ego or awareness to see they're not necessarily their emotion. Emotions are information systems in the body, but they're not always based on fact. If your brother is running late to a meeting you're supposed to be see him at, and you start getting angry about it, supposing that he's being disrespectful or careless, he may have been in a car accident. Anger may be based on something that's completely non-factual.

Our emotions are not factual mechanisms—they're not real—so creating a perceptual position that allows us to observe an emotion without judgment can help us to not be enmeshed or fused with it.

This is the heart of the problem with impulsivity. People believe, "I feel, so I must act," rather than just feeling. The heart of cognitive de-fusion is letting a thought be a thought and letting an emotion be an emotion without judging it, without needing to attach a relational frame or meaning or importance to it, and simply letting what is, be.

With those who have taken the life of others, this makes so much more sense than trying to help them make sense out of it. Unfortunately, there is no sense in war. Unfortunately, there is no sense in the tragedy of a drunk driving accident. Unfortunately, there is no sense in the case of Adlai Stevenson, a twelve-year-old kid accidentally taking the life of the best friend of another twelve-year-old kid.

Regardless of your religious background or faith, the Book of Job has something really interesting to say about this. In the Book of Job, Job suffers all of this loss, and Job's three friends come along and say, "Well, it's because you didn't do this or because you didn't do that," "If you only had thought that," or "If you only had done this."

Job's friends really torment him throughout the entire Book of Job. It's not until the very end of the Book of Job that the young guy comes along and says, "There's something bigger going on than you guys will understand."

The point of the Book of Job is not why good people suffer. The point of the Book of Job is you can't make sense out of things that are really nonsensical. When we're dealing with those who have taken the lives of other people, we're dealing with scenarios that we really can't find a resolution to.

Imagine a therapist saying, "I want you to process this and resolve it." How do you resolve taking the life of another person?

So the approach of contextual psychology simply says, "Accept it." That doesn't mean you like it, you endorse it, you want it to happen, or you hope it happens again. It simply means that you acknowledge it as it is, without judgment, without attaching meaning to it. It's simply seeing it as it is so you can then make a decision as to where you go next.

That leads us to the fourth point. It's the meaning that we give thoughts that leads to distress. Our goal is to take somebody from a non-beneficial meaning. You might say a negative meaning, but we don't like using the word *negative*. The goal is to take somebody from a non-beneficial meaning to a beneficial meaning to actually no meaning at all.

The reason to take it in those directions is because when somebody has a non-beneficial meaning in place, if they walk outside and a tree has fallen on my car, some people's immediate reaction will be "This means I'm going to have a bad day" or "This means God hates me" or something. They have a very non-beneficial meaning attached.

To just release meaning altogether when you're in this resource-scarce state can be kind of challenging. One of the things we do is get them to reframe that into a beneficial meaning: "Well, at least I wasn't in the car" or "At least nobody got hurt."

People say all the time, "Something good is going to come of this." Once they have this resourceful state and beneficial meanings, now we can get them to the point where they can release meanings altogether. By releasing meanings altogether, it just means that a tree fell on my car.

You don't do this in ten minutes with a client. This is a process. You need multiple sessions. It's a training process. If we think about it in a behavioral sense, they are creating meanings in a habitual way. We have a meaning-making system with almost everything in life. We learn that system from somebody, most likely, and we employ that without even thinking about.

If you can get them to think about how they're creating meanings, then we can start to change it. So when they catch themselves with a non-beneficial meaning, they're not supposed to punish themselves. They're just supposed to say, "Okay, I see. What's a beneficial meaning?"

After a while, it's the beneficial meanings that become habitual. Once we get the beneficial meanings to be habitual, then we move to no meanings.

As we explain processes in this book, these are the presuppositions that underlie these processes, which have really been helpful to create a sense of release from the psychological distress, or what Steven Hayes would call the suffering, that they experience.

Relational Frame Theory and Acceptance and Commitment Therapy

A mainstay of contextual psychology, Acceptance and Commitment Therapy is one of our favorite approaches to psychotherapy. Steven Hayes wrote a workbook for clients titled *Get Out of Your Mind and Into Your Life*. He is a researcher at the University of Nevada who began his work looking at how to apply psychotherapy to social anxiety. In the DSM-IV (although not true in the DSM-5), PTSD was under the umbrella of the anxiety disorders, and we see a lot of parallels.

Many of the techniques of Acceptance and Commitment Therapy have been applied to those with post-traumatic stress disorder. One strategy that is particularly effective is based on the idea of Relational Frame Theory.

Simply put, we have an adaptive ability—that is, our minds can relate anything to anything. This is an evolutionary trait that puts us in charge of the planet rather than whales being in charge of the planet or dogs being in charge of the planet. It is our mental capacity for creating relational frames. We're the only animals that do this.

By relational frames, what we mean is we have an experience, a thought, a cue, an awareness, and we can relate it to something else. This is great from a problem-solving evolutionary psychology perspective. It's not really great when we have PTSD, because what happens is your client hears a noise down the hall and the relational frame is, "That must be a robber."

Let's say, for example, living in a rough neighborhood where there were helicopters and gunfights outside every day caused your clients' trauma. One day their door was kicked down, and the building was robbed. People in the apartment were raped, shot, and mutilated. Your client survived this. Now they're in a safe place in an entirely different scenario. It's three, five, maybe fifteen years later, but when your client hears noise down the hall, they instantly feel unsafe or even panicked. The relational frame is arbitrary. It's not based on fact, yet it causes the use of emergency coping strategies, which for some of our clients can actually be a matter of life and death.

Let's talk a little bit about how the human mind works and how acceptance and commitment therapy can help break these relational frames.

Grab a piece of paper. Write down the name of any noun, any object. It can be anything you think of. It can be a car, bus, microphone, table, chair, etc. It can be a balloon. It can be anything you want it to.

Now think of another object, another something, another noun. It can be in the room or not be in the room. We'll use balloon and groundhog.

Here are three questions:

1. How is the first noun like a second noun?
2. How is the first noun better than the second one?
3. How is the first noun the parent of the second noun?

This is an exercise from Steven Hayes's book *Get Out of Your Mind and Into Your Life*. You might have to use your brain a little bit, but come up with an answer. Here's an example of this exercise:

Richard: Dave, how is a balloon like a groundhog?

David: My birthday is in February. Isn't Groundhog Day in February?

Richard: This is how the mind works. It comes up with these arbitrary connections that really aren't based on reality. You thought, "My birthday is in February. That means balloons, and Groundhog Day is in February. So groundhogs have balloons too." Ultimately it all revolves around you. This is an example of how we created an arbitrary relational frame.

The second question: How is a balloon better than a groundhog?

David: It doesn't bite. And I don't even know if groundhogs bite.

Richard: They probably don't, because people are picking them up so they can see if they see their shadows. I don't know. I don't want to find out the hard way.

Here's the difficult one. People tend to have a little bit of difficulty with it, but they always come up with an answer: How is a balloon the parent of a groundhog?

David: A balloon is a product of technology. I thought that technology rules over nature.

Richard: It's an arbitrary relational frame. It doesn't matter if your thought makes any sense or not. What's most important is everybody can always answer this question. How is one thing the parent of another thing?

Now we're getting into logic. Not everything can always be the parent of everything, and yet your mind can create that relational frame.

What happens to our clients with PTSD is they create these arbitrary relational frames: "This means that, and because it means that, I must do this." Albert Ellis famously called this line of thought *musterbation*. Our clients engage in self-defeating behavior because of these rules they set for themselves based on arbitrary relational frames that really don't exist.

Underlying almost all of the strategies and interventions discussed in this book are the presuppositions of contextual psychology, especially Relational Frame Theory. Once we recognize our ability to assign meaning and the fact that assigning meaning leads to suffering, we can free ourselves from the suffering caused by arbitrary frames.

MINDFULNESS

Mindfulness is in many ways the process of applying our understanding of Relational Frame Theory—that is, our understanding that thoughts (and the events observed in our thoughts) do not have meaning until we assign meaning to them. With mindfulness, we learn to simply let a thought be a thought or let an object be an object without attaching a relational frame to it.

Mindfulness is one of the core components of Dialectical Behavioral Therapy and other contextual psychologies, which is why we're devoting a whole chapter to it. When we're dealing with the clients with post-traumatic stress disorder, the research shows that training those clients in mindfulness can help us to bring the clients into the present so that they can avoid revivifying and reliving the past traumas that they have experienced while avoiding the tendency to project those traumas into the future.

The diagnosis of PTSD is made not because the client has intrusive thoughts—it's important to note that–but because the intrusive thoughts cause clinically significant impairment. If we can teach or train a client in an activity that, despite their thoughts or despite their past or despite the horribleness of the scenario, can remove the clinically significant impairment in important areas of functioning, then we are on the road to recovery with that client. Mindfulness is one very effective strategy to do just that.

All thoughts are intrusive. If you know that you are going to be receiving a $500,000 check in the mail next week, that thought can be just as intrusive, just as distracting, and in a way, just as debilitating as the thought of a past trauma.

What if the mail doesn't come? You'd better not go to work. You'd better stand in front of the mailbox. Then your spouse wonders why you are standing out in the rain.

A fish does not know that it's swimming in water. If it got out of the water, it would know that it was missing the water, but as long as a fish stays in the water, which is where fish live, it doesn't know it's in water. It doesn't know there's the City of Tulsa over here, or New York City over there, or Singapore over there. It doesn't even know there's water; the fish just experiences it.

People are figuratively swimming in thoughts the way a fish is swimming in water. A lot of times we think that meditation is about turning off our thoughts. That would be like a fish getting out of the water. It's impossible to stop thinking. That's not what the mind does.

In fact, if we consciously think about not thinking, then we're actually thinking about the thoughts of not thinking, which is actually a thought.

An easy way to help a client who is swimming in their thoughts is to go back to teaching them this strategy for mindfulness—a thought is just a thought, just like water is water for a fish. It doesn't mean anything. It just is.

Mindfulness is a great tool for just about anything. It's great at creating a space. Most people are mindlessly fused with their emotions or enmeshed in their thoughts. Mindfulness creates a habit of de-fusing from our thoughts.

Let's say your client was driving to the office and killed a pedestrian who was crossing the road, and this is now very distressing. What would you tell your client the value of mindfulness is? It's simply breathing in and out. It seems too simple to have any value. How would you share this so that your client would see this as a useful tool?

You might say, "In the distress that has come up, a lot of your suffering isn't from the actual distress. A lot of the distress isn't even from the actual thoughts that come up about killing a person. A lot of the stress is based on being enmeshed or fused with that stress or with those thoughts."

Now a client is going to say, "But they're real thoughts. They're really powerful. It was awful."

Reply, "I understand that." If a client is insisting they're real thoughts, don't say that they're not real thoughts, because to your client, those are real thoughts. And they are real thoughts on a subjective level.

Mindfulness can help your client understand there are perceptual positions, and you can help your client view the thoughts from a new angle. Often it's not the thought "I killed somebody" that distresses your client. It's the thought about the thought: "I killed somebody and that means…" and so we've got a conversation, a new perceptual position and then another perceptual position. Inside our thoughts, we have multiple conversations going on at any time:

"If I was only a more careful driver…"

"If I was only really not texting and driving … I didn't let them know that I was, but…"

"Why did she run that light?"

"Why did he walk across the sidewalk on a busy street without looking for cars?"

"Why did they jaywalk?"

Your client can really get hung up on all these thoughts.

What happens when we have a thought? It doesn't even have to be a thought about killing someone. Suppose we see someone in an expensive suit, and we immediately think he's uptight or greedy. That's a judgment.

Typically one of two things happen. We either enmesh with that thought, which pins it in place and energizes it; or we deny that thought and say, "I shouldn't judge people that way." But that also pins it in place. The focus is still on the thought.

Thoughts and feelings are essentially cerebral farts. They bubble up, and then deciding to stick our face in it makes it worse.

In mindfulness, we practice a concept called noting. The idea is that when a thought arises, we just note it as thought, just like a fish notes it as water. They don't attach meaning to it: "This water is good" or "this water is bad." They just say, "It's water through my gills."

The idea of noting is to really not give importance to any particular thought, but rather to say, "It's a thought," so it passes through the mind like a cloud as opposed to staying in place and raining on us all day long.

The goal of mindfulness, the goal of contextual psychology, is not to erase our memory of bad things or keep from being aware of the future, but to live fully in the present despite where we've been and despite where we're going.

How Can You Teach a Client Mindfulness?

When one of us has a client who is new to our office, we teach them a two-minute mindfulness meditation and then assign them to do a two-minute mindfulness meditation twice a day. We may even give them a short mp3 that teaches them a core strategy for practicing mindfulness. The important thing is that they practice several times a day.

We start them out at two minutes because we find that there's a higher rate of success if we assign two minutes rather than trying to get them to do it for ten, fifteen, or thirty minutes. Attempting longer periods of meditation at the beginning just leads to failure and frustration.

In truth, the value is not in meditating for thirty or forty-five minutes each day. The value lies in internalizing and practicing the processes. If we can do that in two minutes, then we can be mindful twenty-four hours a day. The idea is not that this two minutes is valuable to me, but what I learned in the two minutes, I can then take with me so that when I experience these symptoms of PTSD, I can now bring myself to the present despite my past. Previously, I would have revivified and become enmeshed with the trauma.

Many people hear the word *meditation* and think maybe it's some esoteric or new-agey type of thing. Understand that different types of meditation have been practiced for thousands of years.

There's a type of meditation called focus meditation. That's staring at the candle or whatever. The whole idea is to suppress any thoughts and achieve a state of bliss. That's not a bad way to practice meditation, but it really doesn't have lasting effects once the meditation is done.

The other type of meditation—the type of meditation we're talking about—is mindfulness. It is not suppressing the thought, but it's allowing the thought to arise, noting it as thought, and not becoming enmeshed with it. Usually we use our breath as the anchor.

Your attention is focused somewhere, so as opposed to your attention getting enmeshed in the thought, you allow the thought to be transient—like a cloud—and you note it as a thought, then just go back to focusing on your breathing.

Some people close their eyes during mindfulness meditation. You don't even have to use the word meditation. We can call it a mindfulness exercise. We can call it a practice in staying present. You can reframe this any way you want for your clients.

Some people do like their eyes closed, and that's fine. There's no right or wrong way to do this. One reason to keep your eyes open is that we tend to visualize much more with our eyes closed.

Find a specific point to stare at and let that become your second anchor. Your breath is the first anchor. The point is another anchor. As you breathe, count from one to four as you inhale and then again as you exhale. (When you have more practice, you can release the counting.)

A lot of times you'll start thinking a thought. You will become an active participant. But then there comes a time when you notice that you're thinking and go, "Oh." You note it as a thought and then go back to focusing on your breathing.

A lot of times what we focus on is the area where the air enters the nose. Some people will feel it around their nostrils. Some people will feel it on their lip. But we focus on our breathing, the counting, the spot, and where the air is entering.

This is really a training process. You're teaching a person to practice a ritual that they can do each day so that they can bring their awareness when they're bothered by intrusive thoughts to something as simple as a spot on a table or a breath, just by noting the thought as a thought.

It's not trying to suppress the thought. It's allowing the thought just to rise and go away, because that's what thoughts do.

It seems a lot easier to simply note a thought and let it be a thought, even if it's a distressing thought, then to try and get rid of it. One of the interesting things is thought suppression techniques, which have been popular in therapy, simply aren't effective because that's not the way the mind works.

In fact, there was an old Bob Newhart skit called "Stop It." Bob has a client who's all stressed out. Bob Newhart plays a psychiatrist, and every time his client mentions being stressed, anxious, or fearful, he shouts, "Stop it stop it, stop it!" That doesn't work, though. Thought suppression doesn't work. What really is more effective is going with the thought.

We're going to guide you through a basic process of mindfulness. This is a strategy for paying attention to the present moment, for setting aside the rumination of the past or the anxiety about the future and just being present. By the way, this is highly effective as a strategy for helping clients who have difficulty sleeping.

This is a mindfulness exercise:

Imagine lying on your pillow. Even if you have thoughts, you can just let those thoughts be thoughts and you can just be present with your pillow and you'll find that it becomes easy for you to avoid becoming enmeshed with those regrets or ruminations or those anxieties and projections and can simply sleep. Mindfulness can be a strategy to induce sleep or a strategy for simply living fully in the present.

Go ahead and close your eyes. With the eyes closed, breathe in and breathe out. You don't need to speed up or slow down the breath. Simply breathe. We go through life without usually thinking about the breath, but we've been breathing since the first day of life. We'll continue to breathe until the end of life.

And because the breath is always with us, it's an easy focal point for the present. So as you breathe in, pay attention to the air as it enters the nostrils and what it feels like to breathe the air down the throat and into the lungs. Really follow the breath. Notice that point where the inhale deep in the lungs turns into an exhale. Pay attention to what it feels like to breathe the air out.

Continue breathing, bringing your attention to this moment, this breath. Notice as you pay attention to this breath and this moment, that with each breath, you become fully immersed in this time.

In doing so, of course you set aside the regrets of yesterday, the anticipation or fear of tomorrow, and simply breathe. And if you find yourself thinking about the past or projecting into the future, use your breath as a focal point to return your attention to the present.

As you breathe in and out, if you notice that you have a thought, don't follow that thought. Simply let that thought be a thought, returning your attention to the breath to break that automatic pattern of following that thought.

And if you have a feeling, simply note that feeling. You don't have to try to escape it. Just label it. See it as it is, but return your attention to breath, breathing in, breathing out, being fully present in this moment.

Now go ahead and open your eyes. Breathe in, letting your lungs be filled with oxygen, becoming energized from that breath. Open the eyes if your eyes aren't open.

That's a short two-minute process of mindfulness. This is a very simple strategy for helping your clients to live fully in the present, to simply let a thought be thought, a feeling be a feeling, without becoming enmeshed in it, without falling in.

Going through that process once probably won't solve any problems. Its value is really in a daily practice.

THE SKILL OF FORGIVENESS

In our society, especially in our profession, we want to make everything better. We want to take a pill and undo the past, but that can't be done. The only pill we can take to undo the past is one that makes us forget the past, which we become addicted to, which causes us more problems.

In hypnotherapy, people call up and literally say, "I would like to make an appointment. I want you to hypnotize me to forget the past." Many clients want to block out what has happened.

Too many of our therapeutic approaches often are those that really try to get our clients to forget the past, to not think of the yellow jeep rather than moving them towards acceptance.

We know thought suppression doesn't work because you have to conceptualize the object that you don't want to think of. If you were a tightrope walker and someone kept on yelling, "Don't fall! Don't fall!" you have to conceptualize falling in order to not fall—which makes you more likely to fall. By the way, if you wonder how the Law of Attraction works, this is it. It's not this great metaphysical spiritual truth. The reality is that what we attend to, we consider; what we consider, we eventually act upon.

It's vital when you're working with these clients to really find out what they're attending to on a daily, on an hourly, on a minute-by-minute basis. What are they attending to? Can this thing in the past be minimized to just a thing in the past? Can it be part of the recipe and the rich variety of every human being?

Some people worry that it discounts the importance of having killed to relegate it to simply another life experience, to minimize it. Some people would say, "But this is real. This is so important. This is defining." And it really is.

However, if you go to a wartime culture or warlike culture, the importance of killing really is minimal. In Afghanistan, if you go down to the Waziristan area, they practice their own tribal code. Blood feuds are very common. They don't identify at all with killing somebody. That's something you do when you have a blood feud. In our culture, it is a very big deal.

To Forgive or Not to Forgive

There is a time when forgiveness processes are important and a time when forgiveness processes are contraindicated. Let's talk about when they're contraindicated first.

Obviously, if your client feels justified in the action, forgiveness is contraindicated.

Consider Richard's brother-in-law who served as an infantryman. He volunteered to serve. He served both in Iraq and Afghanistan. He received a Purple Heart. Now he serves as a sheriff deputy. He's done his job very well in the military, and he's done his job very well in civilian life. He knows, without question, that he has taken the life of others on the battlefield.

(With today's technology, a lot of soldiers, unless they've been in close quarters combat, aren't aware as to whether or not they've taken a life. That can be another area of real confusion for them.)

But Richard's brother-in-law has knowledge of the actions that he's taken, and he feels very proud to have done his job well. He has no guilt and no remorse, and he doesn't believe he should. He did exactly what he was supposed to do in order to serve and protect his country, particularly immediately following 9/11. He was one of the first soldiers in Afghanistan in 2002. Forgiveness is not an appropriate route for him.

Likewise, the need for forgiveness may not be readily apparent to the client, and it's important to let your clients reach their own realizations about this. Most people don't present by saying, "I killed somebody, so now I'd like to see a counselor." They call up five, ten, or fifteen years later, or even just two to three months later and say, "Hey, I'm depressed," or "Hey, I can't sleep," or "Hey, I can't figure out why I'm anxious."

Let's say a client presented now, and we discovered that in his history. Of course it wouldn't be too hard to discover because he would tell us exactly what he's been doing the last ten years. We would attach meaning to this and maybe say, "Self-forgiveness is important." Yet, really forgiveness processes would be contraindicated. That's an obvious example.

What are some other examples where forgiveness as a process in therapy would be contraindicated?

If somebody has a criminal background and has killed numerous people, they need to feel shameful or guilty before they can practice forgiveness. Oftentimes, they'll say, "Yeah, I forgive myself. No problem." Then what have they learned as a human being from that experience if they go right into it?

We look at forgiveness as a process when that's what a client needs. But we don't operate on the assumption that all clients who have killed somebody need to forgive themselves.

When we have clients, though, who have identified a need for forgiveness, they'll tell us. Here are some interesting things about forgiveness: It actually increases productivity. It increases health.

The Journal of Professional Psychology reported in a study of fifty-nine counseling clients, therapists who used specific forgiveness interventions were more successful than those who did not. That doesn't mean every client is an appropriate candidate, but one of the things we should be looking for is our clients letting us know what their needs are.

Twelve Steps to Forgiveness

In his book *Forgiving and Reconciling: Bridges to Wholeness and Hope*, Dr. Everett Worthington recommends twelve steps to becoming a more forgiving person:

1. Reflect on WHY you want to be more forgiving.
2. Identify your greatest wounds from the past.
   In the case of a soldier who may have killed many times—sometimes having killed civilians by accident or on purpose, having killed in self-defense, having killed through friendly fire—put a hierarchy on the deaths.
3. Forgive ONE wound at a time.
4. Identify Heroes of Forgiveness (such as Gandhi, Nelson Mandela, or Solzhenitsyn) and model their behavior.
5. Examine yourself.
6. Reduce negative traits; cultivate virtue.
   Say, "If I were more _____, I would _____ more often."
7. Change your experience of the past.
   You cannot change what happened, but you can change your perception of what happened, you can change your emotional and mental associations of what happened,

> *and you can change your understanding of the meaning of the event.*

8. Plan your self-improvement strategy.
   Ask yourself, "What can I do to better myself, despite where I've been before?"
9. Practice forgiving under imagined conditions.
10. Practice forgiving day-to-day.
11. Seek help from someone you trust.
    Your friends or spouse may not be objective, so use a professional.
12. Start a campaign to love your enemies.

This is a process that can help a person become forgiving and experience a sense of reconciliation.

Changing Perceptual Position

One other really solid technique for helping a person acquire a sense of forgiveness, particularly towards themselves, is to come up with somebody that they know, whether currently in their life or from before, who loved them and who would forgive them for basically anything.

If you can have them close their eyes and visualize standing in front of that person and allow their consciousness to rise above themselves and float into the other person so they're actually seeing themselves through the other person's eyes and allow them to feel the forgiveness that would well up inside the other people and the love that would well up inside the other person, it will give them an opportunity to experience that from a completely different perceptual position.

Let's talk a minute about perceptual position. Perceptual position is important.

First Perceptual Position: Seeing through your own eyes, from your perspective.

Second Perceptual Position: Seeing through the eyes of another person, typically a person you are interacting with.

Third Perceptual Position: Seeing the situation "from above," as a neutral observer free from a participant's filters.

Another way of putting it is I can be me as me; I can be me outside of me observing me; or I can be me outside of me and me outside of the outside me watching me watch me, if that makes sense.

This is an important concept in NLP. When our clients, particularly our PTSD clients, are experiencing distress, they are seeing themselves from the vantage point of the first perceptual position. This is what the revivification of PTSD is. They become re-traumatized in the safety of the office, which makes no sense because the event was ten years ago, because every cue, every environmental awareness, every subconscious awareness retriggers the experience of reliving something as an enmeshed "me."

Much like practicing mindfulness, training our clients to move to the second or third perceptual position, a dissociative state (which is far different than dissociative personality disorder) outside of themselves puts a buffer between them and the event.

If you're having a client look at or describe an event that's difficult, you can have them imagine themselves in a movie theater watching a movie of themselves. That's the third perceptual position, a dissociated position.

If that's uncomfortable for them, you might even have them be an outside observer watching them watch themselves. That's called "double-dissociation." We can use these perceptual positions to effect changes therapeutically.

Another process is one of entering the second perceptual position—seeing from another's vantage point. For example, Hal's grandmother was the most forgiving person on the planet. One day Hal had a conflict with his mother, and his grandmother, who was probably ninety years old at the time, said, "Don't worry. I'll knock her off her high horse." It was hilarious, because at ninety she wasn't going to be doing much knocking at all.

But Hal's grandmother always forgave him unconditionally and always had his back. So he can go into a second perceptual position, seeing himself from his grandmother's eyes, to develop a sense of self-forgiveness.

We have all forgiven somebody at one point in time somewhere along the way, so we know what forgiveness feels like inside of our body. We often say, "I can't forgive myself." What that really means is, "I want to open the gates inside of me to allow me to feel forgiveness."

When we create this new perceptual position and we guide our client into somebody who we know would forgive them, it allows those gates to open. In a way, we're tricking them into opening those gates and allowing themselves to feel a state, an emotion that they don't know how to feel. It almost tricks them into creating an experience that's of value to them.

Loving-Kindness Meditation

We want to go through a process of a loving-kindness meditation. This is probably a 5,000-year-old process. It's something we teach some of our clients because it's an appropriate practice for becoming forgiving and loving.

Remember, our deepest spiritual need is to love other people and to feel worthy of receiving love in return. A lot of our clients who have taken the lives of other people find that by practicing this loving-kindness meditation, they can actually cultivate a sense of loving and kindness. Even in situations where they grew up as criminals, they have been in traumatic battle zones, or they have engaged in conduct that has disregarded the safety of others, we can bring them to a new place today.

Read through this process and then practice it yourself:

Close your eyes down. Focus on your breath: breathing in, breathing out, and setting aside any worry about the past or anxiety about the future. Simply attend to the present.

The practice always begins with developing a loving acceptance of yourself. Sometimes resistance experienced simply indicates feelings of unworthiness might be present. But you don't have to worry about that because this means that there's work to be done. The practice that we're going to do is actually designed to help you overcome any feelings of self-doubt or negativity.

So as you breathe in and as you breathe out, with each breath allow yourself to become fully present in this moment. Now think about a person. Identify a person who is a respected or beloved person you are aware of— maybe a teacher or a spiritual guide who has been important to you—a mentor. Or even somebody who, although you haven't known them personally, on the world stage is a person who you may find carries the traits of being a beloved and respected person.

Now that you have identified that person, allow yourself to enter that resource state of feeling a sense of loving-kindness towards that person, that person who has taught you—maybe an author or a wise teacher or example from history.

Notice how it's easy for you to feel a sense of loving-kindness towards that person, especially if they've given much back to our world.

Let's personalize this a little bit. Think of a dearly beloved person. It could be a close family member or friend, somebody who is dearly loved by you.

And as you breathe in and breathe out, allow yourself to sense loving-kindness directed towards that person. Again, it's an easy and natural thing for us to do. Most people have no difficulty with this.

The third category is a neutral person, just somebody in your world—somebody who you know, but you've never thought about having any special feelings towards. Maybe it's a person who serves you in a shop, or somebody in your office, or somebody you know from the neighborhood.

It's amazing how as you identify this person, breathing in and breathing out, you can actually allow yourself to feel a sense of loving-kindness towards this person, even though until this moment you've never ascribed any special status to that person. Continue to feel it as you breathe in, breathe out.

Now think of a hostile person: a person in your world whom you've had difficulty with, whom the idea of loving or even feeling kindness towards has been difficult. Once you identify this person, in this moment, breathe in and breathe out, having practiced a feeling—a sense of loving—extend this loving-kindness to this fourth category of person, to this person toward whom you felt hostility or difficulty.

It's amazing to note, as you breathe in and breathe out, how by breathing in love and exhaling kindness, you can extend those same feelings that you easily did to the others towards this person as well.

Of course depending on the client we're working with, we may include a fifth category—and that is themselves. Breathing in, breathing out, and letting themselves feel love, kindness, and acceptance towards oneself.

Allowing yourself right now to feel a sense of loving-kindness and acceptance towards yourself just as you were able to do with others as well. It feel awesome, doesn't it?

Take in a breath and let that oxygen fill your lungs. Let that oxygen rejuvenate every cell of the body. And as you open the eyes feeling fantastic, recognize that you just learned a basic process for training a person to experience the resource state, which is really what loving-kindness is. It can help you problem-solve and become more forgiving not only of others, but of yourself as well, regardless of previous difficult life experiences.

The importance of the loving-kindness meditation is that no matter where a client is and no matter what your client has or has not done, probably the most beneficial thing that we can help a client cultivate is a very gentle approach to themselves.

Similarly, as a therapist, the most beneficial thing that you can do for your client is to cultivate a gentle approach to yourself. We find it a lot easier to help our clients when we actually do what we ask our clients to do.

Your clients are going to model you, typically. There can be the real fighter attitude of "We're going to solve this problem" and that's a beneficial attitude. But if we approach everything, particularly ourselves, in a manner of just gentle acceptance and a curious nature about who we are as a human being, that's going to play out in every way with our own client.

The idea of loving-kindness really starts with us. There's a Buddhist nun named Pema Chodron, and she writes about it a great deal. She talks about cultivating an unconditional friendship with yourself.

This is something that we can take to heart, and this is something that we can encourage our clients to do. The simple fact is they can't go back and change anything that's happened. But if they have time-bound themselves, if they have defined themselves by that act, then they may need to develop that unconditional friendship with the self.

Modeling Self-Forgiveness for Your Clients

Cultivate a gentle approach with yourself first. Sometimes when we sit in front of a client, we don't know all the answers, and we don't know how to help them create relief in that very moment.

We often tell clients, "What you're telling me is really awful. I don't know how to make it better. But what I do know how to do is help you to be present in this moment."

That's vital. We can take the content of anything, and if we reframe it to a whole different structure, to a whole different context, that changes the meaning we assign to it.

In the event of somebody who has killed, we go and find meaning. What is that meaning? Would it mean that same thing in every other situation? If there is forgiveness that's needed, if they do need to forgive themselves, if they do need to forgive their parents, if they do need to forgive the society that turned them into a killer, then there's a process for forgiveness.

If they don't need to forgive themselves, why would we force that upon them? As a therapist, you have a role of authority, so if you tell them something, chance are they're going to believe you.

Even if you're just being kind to them, you're saying, "Wow, I know that's really a horrible thing. You're not a horrible person, but that's really a horrible thing." If they've never thought that it was a horrible thing before, now you've given them a whole new line of suffering.

We can't avoid pain, but suffering is optional.

Modeling Acceptance for Your Clients

An important step in helping your clients to experience forgiveness is curbing your own natural proclivity to assign blame or guilt.

Richard had a graduate school professor who prided himself on being utterly unflappable. He was a Ministerial Doctor, an LPC, and a Baptist minister for 30 years, so he prided himself on being a Rogerian who learned how to hear anything without raising an eyebrow. That's how he measured therapeutic skill: "Can I hear anything without raising an eyebrow?"

He spent quite a bit of time in graduate school teaching his students how to manifest advanced accurate empathy by listening without raising an eyebrow. He should have been a poker instructor.

We can model loving-kindness and acceptance towards our clients by not raising an eyebrow, by not responding emotionally from our biases. One of the things we need to do is make sure that we do the things that take care of ourselves so that we're able to do this with our clients.

Richard had worked with sex offenders for a couple of years when he was providing training for a group of social workers in South Texas. He mentioned his work in the sex offender treatment program, and one of the social workers said, "Oh, my gosh, how can you work with those people?"

Richard had never thought about it before. He could work with those people because he got a paycheck. At the time, he had young kids, and he really liked being able to pay his rent and car payment, and that was the job he got. He never thought about how he could work with those people.

Richard said, "Well, it's easy for me. I get a paycheck to do it."

"I could never work with those people," the social worker answered.

His response was, "Then you shouldn't."

It's important for us as counselors to recognize what our limits are. It's okay to say, "To work with a population of prisoners because they chose to commit crimes and they're actually proud that they did—that is not something I have the capacity to do." You are allowed to say, "I've become so emotionally invested in the soldiers who have been put in situations where we wouldn't hope anyone to be put into that I can't separate myself from it." It's okay to say, "I'd do best with a different type of client."

That goes into approaching yourself in a gentle way. We may not know what a client feels like who has killed a person. We may not know what a client feels like who has been addicted to drugs or whatever else. But if we remove the exact content of their suffering, then we can appreciate their suffering based on our knowledge of our own suffering.

We don't have to kill somebody to counsel people who have killed people. Suffering is suffering. Pain is pain. And we can't avoid pain, but we can choose to not exacerbate our clients' suffering.

HYPNOTHERAPY

We mention hypnosis, hypnotherapy, and hypnotic processes in the context of a few of the other techniques. In Edna Foa's book, she has a whole chapter dedicated to the efficacy of hypnotherapy. Unfortunately, those who do not have a background or training in Ericksonian or other approaches in hypnosis often perceive it as something strange, bizarre, or mystical.

The reality is that hypnosis is a training tool. In 2008 Richard did an all-day educational conference for American Counseling Association. It was called "Skill Building Hypnosis" because hypnosis actually teaches clients something that they need to know—how to take physical control over their bodies.

There are a lot of different ways to go about inducing hypnosis or utilizing hypnotherapy, but the simplest and often most effective methods uses breathing work and progressive muscle relaxation. Many therapists, even though they don't call themselves hypnotists, are using hypnotic methods of visualization, deep breathing, and progressive muscle relaxation.

When we lead a formal process of hypnosis, we're actually teaching a self-soothing strategy for managing anxiety as well as the physical distress that come along with post-traumatic stress disorder.

We'll often incorporate and utilize autogenic training. Most people hear of autogenic training and say, "What's that?" It's interesting. A technique was developed in 1928 called progressive muscle relaxation by Edmund Jacobson—Jacobson's progressive muscle relaxation: Tense and relax, tense and relax. In 1932, a German cardiologist named Schultz came up with the idea of autogenic training, and the two really pair together well.

Richard learned autogenic training from the nurses on the psychiatric unit where he first worked during graduate school. It's interesting that in the world of therapy we don't spend too much time talking about autogenic training as an idea, but the world of nursing certainly has utilized that idea.

A Simple Hypnotic Induction

Both PMR and autogenic training are hypnotic processes, and we use them in formal hypnotic inductions. The following process is a fine example. Read through it a few times and then guide yourself through the process, or make a recording of it and listen to it:

> Go ahead and close your eyes and relax in a chair. Take in a breath, breathing in and breathing out. You don't have to speed up or slow down your breath, but with each breath allow yourself to set aside any tension of yesterday or stress about tomorrow and focus on this moment. Feel the chair below you and hear my voice.

> As you breathe in and breathe out, with each breath allow yourself to relax a little more deeply. Never asleep, of course, and you can always hear my voice, but deeply relaxed.

> The tension of the day is often held in the brow, the muscles of the eyes and the muscles of the cheeks. You can relax those muscles. You can let those eyelids become relaxed. You may have heard a hypnotist out of Hollywood say, "Your eyes are getting sleepy." That's because when you relax them, those eyelids simply become heavy and relaxed.

As you relax in the chair with your eyes closed, unclench the jaw. Let the jaw relax. You can even let that chin drop towards the chest, letting the muscles in the neck and shoulders relax, the muscles in the arms relax. And it's kind of fun to notice how relaxed you can actually let yourself become as you breathe in and breathe out.

Notice how relaxed the little tiny muscles in the hands resting on your lap can become. As the muscles in the hands and palms relax, notice how heavy the hands become, kind of like the eyelids. In fact, you can even say to yourself, "My hands are heavy; my hands are heavy."

And let those hands experience heaviness as they relax. Think of warmth: warmth like that which might come from the sun or even from inside of the body. And pay attention to your hands and say to yourself, "My hands are warm and heavy; my hands are warm and heavy," and let those hands become both warm and heavy as they relax, saying to yourself, "My hands are warm and heavy."

Notice that feeling of warmth, that feeling of heaviness. In fact, so heavy that if you try to lift your hands, you'll find they're simply so heavy it's more comfortable to let them simply sit on your lap. Trying to lift your hands but find they become heavier and heavier and just resting on your lap.

As you breathe in and breathe out, let that relaxation spread through the belly and back and buttocks and thighs, into the calves and the shins. And even the little tiny muscles of the toes and feet. It feels good to let them relax, too.

As you breathe in and breathe out note the difference between the tension of the day and the state of relaxation that you have created here and now. This isn't a state that I have given you or that a drug has induced, but simply a state of creative relaxation that you have created yourself by going through a process of progressive muscle relaxation, autogenic training, and simply paying attention to your breath.

Notice how wonderful it feels to simply take a minute during a stressful and busy day to center yourself, lean something new, and feel awesome. At any time over the next day or two or three, you find yourself caught up in the stress of the moment, you can anywhere close your eyes for a moment, take in a breath and bring yourself instantly back to this state that you've created right here and right now.

But because this is only a brief demonstration, go ahead and pay attention to the floor below you and the air in the room around you. Take in a breath and get ready to open the eyes. When I count to three, open the eyes and feel fantastic. One, two, three—opening the eyes.

That was a very short and abbreviated process, but it felt pretty awesome, didn't it? Notice the difference between the tension you had just ten minutes ago and how calm you feel right now.

This is a skill that we can actually teach clients. When you have clients who have, as the DSM-5 points out, physiological symptoms of PTSD, you can use progressive muscle relaxation and autogenic training. Autogenic training is the warmth and heaviness. It's the sensorial. There was no sun in the room. There was no difference in your body temperature, but when you said to yourself, "My hands are warm and heavy," they became warm and heavy.

Here's what you want your client to silently ask: "If I can create warmth and heaviness in my hands, can I create calm and serenity in my heart or a sense of safety and security even when I hear a loud noise outside of the room?" The answer is yes.

By teaching a client the processes of self-hypnosis—all hypnosis is self-hypnosis—in a formal process like this, we can really teach them another form of skill-building that the research actually shows is truly useful.

Metaphor in Hypnosis

A state of hypnosis isn't a state of unconsciousness or being zapped. That's too much Hollywood. It's really just a method of accessing the creative and intuitive part of the mind so that we can utilize what are called indirect suggestions: metaphors, stories, and parables.

Metaphor is an important part of acceptance and commitment therapy. It's really an important part of the hypnosis work as well.

When somebody gives us a metaphor, they're giving us their model on how they see things. There are multiple ways of working with metaphors. You can either utilize the client's metaphor or you can create a metaphor for the client.

If you're working with a client's metaphor, you can turn that metaphor into a number of different things. If a client says, "I'm at the end of my rope," they're giving you a metaphor. They feel literally as if they're at the end of the rope.

If you were to examine that metaphor, you could say, "Okay. Well, how far down is it to the ground?" or "Can you climb back up the rope?"

If they say, "I'm hitting a wall," you can ask, "How high is the wall? How far or wide is the wall? What is around the wall? Is there a ladder near? Can we create a ladder?"

Clients will give you their model of the world in metaphors.

In a state of hypnosis, when your client goes through an induction like that and now he's thinking in metaphors, this is the only thing he's focused on and it can really give him a vantage point that he's never had before.

By the way, you do not have to be naturally gifted at coming up with metaphors. There are a lot of useful tools for therapists. There's a book called *Therapeutic Metaphors* by David Gordon. It's simply an encyclopedia of metaphors that a therapist might use to guide, teach, and instruct a client.

You can also concretize your client's metaphors. A client who is having difficulties at work might tell you, "It's just like being hit in the face with a baseball bat." So make that concrete: "Yes, I am sure that it's just like being hit in the face with a baseball bat."

If you think of the psychological suffering that's going on, your client is suffering at the level of being hit in the face with a baseball bat because of their story. When I say, "Yes, it's just like being hit in the face with a baseball bat," then the client says, "Well, maybe it's like being hit in the face with a wiffle ball bat." There's a relief that's given from them changing their metaphor. That's concretization.

One reason metaphors and stories are so successful is that if your clients come to see you and you simply tell them what to do, they might not accept it. But if you tell a story, your client can identify with the character in the story and choose to take alternative action. In other words, metaphors and stories bypass your clients' inherent rejection of new ideas.

Why do you think all religions use parables as teaching tools? Faith leaders don't just tell you what to do. They tell stories. That takes hold—and that's really the essence of hypnosis.

SUBMODALITY SHIFTING

One of the most distressing things for those who have experienced a traumatic event, such as having taken the life of another, are the chronic, recurrent, or ever-present mental pictures related to the event. In some ways it may be reliving, a revivification, but many times these intrusive mental pictures almost like a daydream: They're at their desk, they're simply doing their job counting widgets or whatever is they do, and these intrusive mental pictures come. When we have somebody in our office who has these experiences, what can we do with them?

Different people will experience this differently, so there's not really one common reaction. Some people will have very vivid mental images, and some people have very intense physical bodily sensations. Depending on whether it's a mental image or a physical sensation, a lot of times if we address the symptom itself instead of trying to solve a massive problem, such as PTSD or living with the memory of having taken a life, we may be able to affect at least some sort of relief to that one symptom. We shouldn't overlook or downplay how much impact symptom relief can have on a client's happiness and wellbeing.

Submodality Shifting is a technique used in the branch of hypnotherapy called Neuro-Linguistic Programming (NLP). It aims specifically at symptom relief.

In a nutshell, Submodality Shifting has two steps:

1. Become very curious about how your client experiences the problem.
2. See if you can change how they experience it.

This is most easily demonstrated with a role-playing example we used in our live workshops.

Client: I own some rural land in rural Oklahoma, and I've had something traumatic happen to me there. My friend and I were out on my property, and the neighbor didn't fence off his bulls, and the bull came across the field because it saw we were wearing red t-shirts, and the bull gored my friend. We both ran from the bull, and I was able to get away, but he was gored through the back and killed there on my land.

Now if I'm at work and I see a red pen on the desk, suddenly I remember those red t-shirts, and the bull goring my friend, and the red blood everywhere. When I drive my car, I see a stop sign, and there it is again— the red t-shirts and the red blood and the bull.

That's my intrusive mental image. I try to sleep at night, and nothing happens with that.

Therapist: When you see red, is it just the red, or does the image of that event of your friend getting gored come back?

Client: It's really an image almost like I'm watching a still picture of us right when that bull is getting him. I can see me, and I can see him.

[This is one of the things to look for when people are describing an image or experience: The client described a snapshot from the Third Perceptual Position, so the therapist is going to work with a snapshot, finding out what elements can be changed.

Note that the therapist doesn't point out that bulls are color-blind, so the red shirts probably had nothing to do with the event; the therapist does not approach an irrational association from a rational standpoint.]

Therapist: When you see that snapshot, when you're looking straight ahead, in your field of view, where do you see that?

Client: It's always just right in front.

Therapist: It's always right in front of you right there. Okay. Is it there with your eyes open and your eyes closed?

Client: Yeah.

Therapist: Is it in color, or is it black and white?

Client: It's in color. It's very real. It's like I'm just taking a picture.

Therapist: *(gesturing in front of the client)* When it's here and when you see it, what do you feel?

Client: I feel a lot of anxiety.

Therapist: And where do you feel anxiety?

Client: It starts right here *(points to chest)* and I just feel…

Therapist: And on a scale of zero to ten, how strongly do you feel that anxiety when you see that picture?

Client: Like an eight or nine—sometimes a ten. Sometimes I'm just like, "Whoa!" I close my eyes and make it go away.

Therapist: So closing your eyes makes it go away?

Client: Sometimes.

Therapist: Okay, good.

Client: But I can't really get it to stop.

Therapist: Okay. I want you look straight ahead and look at that picture, and I want you to imagine actually moving that picture closer and see if you increase your level of anxiety or decrease it. See what happens.

Client: Close my eyes?

Therapist: You can keep them open or close them—however you see it best. Just move it closer.

Client: Okay.

Therapist: Does that increase or decrease your anxiety or do things stay the same?

Client: I can feel it getting worse.

Therapist: So now if we move it back to its original position, push it back to its original position, now what happens with your anxiety?

Client: It's not quite as bad.

Therapist: I want you to move it back to about here. *(gestures farther away)* What does that do for your anxiety?

Client: It makes it smaller.

Therapist: Okay. I want you to move it back to about here then. *(gestures even farther away)* What does it do now?

Client: I still feel anxious, but it's not really as anxious. It's not as anxious as I thought just a minute ago when it was in the original position.

Therapist: What I want you to do now is, looking right here, I want you to imagine moving the picture—without following it—moving the picture over to here.

(gestures to across the room) What does that do for your anxiety?

Client: It decreases it quite a bit—I'd say it's down to a three on that scale.

Therapist: Okay, good.

What we're dealing with here is changing the submodalities, the sensorial experience of your client's emotion. The client describes the sensory aspects of the emotion. So the client tells you which modality they experience the emotion in: Is it something they hear, feel, or see?

Then you ask about and start changing the submodalities, which are the parameters within each sensory system. For instance, the submodalities for a visual image include texture, size, shape, closeness, and distance.

For sound, the side of the head it's on, the voice it's in, and the loudness are submodalities to examine. For a feeling, if they say, "I've got anxiety in my chest," ask what does that feel like? What shape is it? What color is it? Is it moving? What direction is it moving?

Shifting the submodalities can give your clients, if not resolution, then symptom relief.

When you guide a client through this process, you help the client to have a sense of control over the symptom, which can be a very freeing experience. Of course, you may not achieve 100% symptom relief, but that's all right. It's okay if it's still there because they have control over it.

Now, in a typical exercise, the intent is to actually increase the anxiety just a little bit. That was the point of moving it closer. The goal is to always have them increase the discomfort before you have them decrease it because people are more willing typically to increase their pain. But if you tell them to decrease it, they'll tell you they can't.

So you have them increase the intensity of the vision, of the sound, of the feeling—take it from an eight to a nine—then you say, "Okay. Now that you know you have control of it, now take it back down to where it was." Then they take it back down to where it was. Now you've just shown them they can turn it up and down, and now you can turn it further down.

However, some clients will respond differently. Some will say that it gets better as it gets closer. Others will find that distance makes no difference, but flattening from three dimensions to two dimensions, or making a color picture black-and-white, will alleviate the symptom.

You get to be inventive with this technique, and you can enjoy improvising. For instance, your client might say that the image comes up like a poster picture, which means that it's very two-dimensional and he can see; in that case, you might have him actually reach up with his hands and rip it or wad it up and drop it in a garbage can.

Again, we don't have to go all the way to zero. Hypnosis practitioners do a lot of pain control. One of the things about pain control is that people in chronic pain will come into the office and says they're at a level ten, and if they can't get anything done, they will become suicidal over their chronic pain. If this technique can get them down to an eight in chronic pain, that 20% reduction is the difference they need to keep going. If they can move to a level eight, maybe in successive sessions we can move to a six or a four.

So this method can help alleviate not only physical pain, but psychological pain, emotional pain, distressing images, and disturbing thoughts.

EMOTIONAL FREEDOM TECHNIQUE

It's really important we begin to think outside of the box with some of the clients who are extremely difficult and have tremendous problems. When we talk to therapists about intervention strategies and ideas, of all of the evidence-based strategies available, the one they are always least familiar with seems to be the Emotional Freedom Technique (EFT). One reason is perhaps that there's debate concerning why EFT works; however, there is no debate around the fact that it does work.

Let's talk a little bit about the research concerning the efficacy of EFT before we discuss theories of how it works. You can go to scholar.google.com and type in "Emotional Freedom Technique (or EFT) and anxiety," or "EFT and [any symptom] relief," or "EFT and post-traumatic stress disorder," and you'll find a tremendous amount of evidence as to its efficacy with a wide range of patient populations.

This isn't one of those areas where we say, "I wonder if this works. Let's try it." We have the studies that demonstrate its efficacy. Of course, there isn't anything that fixes all clients all the time. If we had such interventions, we would be pharmacists, and everyone would be out of business. But occasionally, there are things that can be useful with some clients. The research actually shows that EFT is one of those tools.

The Research

In a Staffordshire University study, twenty-five participants were a sample of third-year, foundation-degree-level, complementary therapy students undertaking a research module. They determined the Subjective Units of Distress (SUD) and the Hospital Anxiety and Depression Scale (HADS) scores for these subjects. Once they determined that, they did EFT. The end result was a significant reduction in SUDs and HADS Anxiety Subscale.

A study in the *Journal of Nervous and Mental Disease* from June of 2011 compares EMDR to EFT. Essentially it finds that both of them are effective in PTSD. A total of forty-six participants that were split between the EMDR and the EFT were assessed at baseline, reassessed at eight weeks, and then at a three-month follow up. Overall the results indicated that both interventions produced significant therapeutic gains.

That's a great phrase to look for when you're reading an abstract or a journal article: *produced significant gains*. That's quite different from what you see in many journal articles: *statistically insignificant differences between the control group and the test group.*

Numerous studies have shown the efficacy of 4-10 sessions of EFT for both substandard PTSD and clinical PTSD. Though the efficacy is well established, there is considerable controversy over how EFT operates.

Competing Theories

Gary Craig created the Emotional Freedom Technique in 1993. He based it on a treatment system, or an energy psychology system, that was already out there called Thought Field Therapy.

Thought Field Therapy was a system of tapping on different energy meridians, the same ones used in acupressure and acupuncture. It was very complex.

Gary Craig said, "I found that these certain points are the one that seems to always work. We don't need to create these formulas based on the presenting symptoms that the client is giving us."

So one explanation for EFT is that there may be something to Chinese medicine. Those who believe in acupuncture and acupressure will find that EFT is based on the same principles.

Alternatively, it could be that it's simply ritual and rapport. We're giving our clients a ritual that provides an excuse to resolve their symptoms. Some view EFT as a hypnotic process, so it may achieve its ends through suggestion and ritual.

The other thing is there's research that indicates that any sensory stimulation above the torso applied to the upper body can disrupt the emotional elements of a memory. There's actually some very interesting evidence. Dr. Melvin Harper in *Traumatology* (December 15, 2011) posted a paper that said that animal and human studies have shown that the emotional aspects of fear memories mediated in the lateral nucleus of the amygdala can be extinguished by the application of low frequency tetanic stimulation (the contraction of muscles) or by repetitive sensory stimulation, such as tapping the cheek.

It sounds a lot like EMDR in the repetitive visual stimulation – which by the way we see in hypnosis too, the eye fixation, or even the bilateral sound waves that can be used for repetitive stimulation.

We always think back to the movie *Airplane* when the woman was in hysterics and the long line of people gathered to help her. What was the old treatment for somebody in hysteria? Slap them.

That's kind of interesting when you think that sensory input will mediate fear.

Here's a fascinating quote from that article: "Nearly all sensory inputs applied to the upper body result in wave power sufficiently large to quench fear memory networks, regardless of input location and type and whether the sensory input is applied unilaterally or bilaterally."

People, a lot of times, when they self-soothe, they'll do the things that we talk about—the physical or sensory input above the torso. That's self-soothing.

There are so many modalities that are like EFT but different. You have havening, which rubs the arms and the face. You have somatic experiencing. A lot of these address the whole body-mind issue of trauma—the idea that trauma is stored in the peptides and not in our normal memory channels. There are a lot of different modalities, but all this goes back to the Harper study in *Traumatology*.

Harper's theory is not that energy meridians cause the change. That may have been the ancient explanation for why this works. It's interesting how sometimes we get the technique that produces change correct, even if our belief as to why that change occurs is not correct.

Sometimes when we notice something we relate it to whatever we have—the cultural and historical awareness that we have at the time.

One view is that most therapy is actually ritual, that when clients come into your office and you've never met them before—the purpose of therapy is often to ratify a change which has already taken place. They were in enough pain to make the call. They made the call. They made the appointment. They took a day off. They came over to your office. They showed up.

Your job really is not to create change because, by doing that process, they've already committed to a path of change. It's your job to simply ratify that change and teach them how to continue in that process of change.

A lot of therapists were taught to talk to people. They do a talk therapy ritual. When we teach a therapist to train a client in a skill like EFT where it's very kinesthetic—they're tapping, they're touching, they're becoming involved in the process—a lot of therapists say, "This is too different for me. This is a ritual I'm not familiar with it."

First off, we know that rapport can be the number one indicator of success in any type of modality. There's a lot of talk these days about empowerment. It's a very catchy term. What a lot of people who use the word "empowerment" don't do is define what empowerment is. The way we define empowerment is to give choice, to give options. When we empower a client, we're basically giving them a choice and options where they no longer knew they had any.

Empowerment is the same whether you work in PTSD, or work with people who've taken a life, or you're a marriage and family therapist working with a couple to empower that couple to give them new choices that they never knew they had in how they relate to each other.

Sometimes when we introduce an idea like this or mindfulness meditation or self-hypnosis training, we'll simply say to our clients, "Sometimes by acknowledging the absurdity of the experience, we can improve it." That helps build rapport.

You can even say, "I know you've been to therapy before, and you've attempted several solutions to resolve this pain. It's really kind of interesting. There's some research to indicate that taking an approach that doesn't just intellectually look at the problems, but actually involves you physically in a process, can help you make change. Although it looks kind of silly"—I'll acknowledge that aspect to my clients—"the research indicates the value in actually learning this process. If you'd like to learn that strategy that a lot of other people have found helpful, I'd be more than happy to teach it to you."

By you saying that, you make it their choice to learn something useful to them. That's a great strategy for introducing it. It's something that they can do on their own when they're not in the office.

Homework is vital to therapy. Every client who comes to see us for therapy, no matter what the presenting problem is, every one of them gets homework assignments. The reason why is they live in a world where there are a lot of things vying for their attention and they'll forget to focus on the task of change between now and the next session, which may be a week later or ten days later, maybe even a month later. By giving homework assignments, if it's not the energy meridians, it's the constant awareness of the process of change.

When we look at PTSD, it's a habit of having these intrusive thoughts. If you ask a combat veteran or an emergency room doctor or a paramedic or somebody else about a particularly bad event, they may talk about it, they may revivify it a little bit, they may get emotional about it, but the difference is they don't do it frequently so it's not a habit for them to do it.

If we think of the cognitive errors and persistent intrusive thoughts as habits, then the thing that people who suffer from PTSD have, that another person going through the exact same thing does not have, is a habit.

One of the other reasons EFT may be effective is because it's a pattern-interrupt. It breaks the daily pattern of depression, intrusive recollection, paranoia, and dissociation with something very specific and very present—similar to what mindfulness does.

The EFT Process

How do you teach basic EFT processes?

The first thing we ask is "What is the problem?" If somebody comes in with PTSD, PTSD isn't the problem. The things that lead them to believe they have PTSD—or lead you to diagnose PTSD—are the problems.

Often they'll respond, "The problem is I can't sleep; the problem is I have intrusive thoughts of a bull goring my neighbor; my wife is going to leave me because I am paranoid and asking her to do things that are out of the ordinary in response to my own fears."

They may have a list of problems. We would typically deal with each one of these symptoms individually. We're going to rate the level of Subjective Units of Distress (SUDs). We're going to rate the SUDs, from zero to ten with zero being not at all and ten being the highest. We're going to ask them to rate it at the moment they're feeling it. This is basically a self-report.

Self-reports are great, because what's most important is the client's experience. When you do a lot of pain control work, the clients you work with have been to zillions of doctors and may even have had surgeries, and in the end the doctors basically say, "It's all in your head. Go see a therapist." They show up in the office, and they really feel crazy. They say, "This really is pain, but they can't find a cause."

That's why the nursing definition of pain is useful. The nursing definition of pain is that pain is whatever the patient says is pain. Subjective measures give useful information.

So when starting the EFT process, if your client says their distress is at (for instance) two, you actually want them to revivify it a little bit. You want to increase that anxiety level because you want something that you can test.

From neurolinguistic programming we have the model of TOTE, which stands for test, operate, test, exit. It's really test, operate, test, operate, test, operate, test, operate, test, operate, test, exit. The idea is we want the client to be in an elevated state to see if we can reduce it through this means. One, that lets us know that this is effective for them. Two, it lets them know that it's effective for them. If they feel it's effective in your office, they're more likely to go home and practice it. Give them the assignment of doing it once a day or twice a day, or when the symptom presents itself.

Then we get the client to describe the situation, the feeling, the pain in the fullest detail they can while using all the sensory input, while using all the metaphors and everything else. We want to have a complete understanding of how they're experiencing this. In the submodalities chapter, we discuss all the different aspects to look for in the description.

Next we need to find the first meridian point. It's a sore spot just below the collarbone. It's sort of a divot above the pectoral muscle. The reason it's sore typically is because of lymphatic drainage. We're going to rub that spot and repeat the affirmation.

This is the affirmation that we give: "Even though I _________ (whatever the problem is), I deeply and completely accept myself." It could be "Even though I feel this pain," or "Even though I see repetitive pictures," or "Even though I don't sleep at night," or "Even though I'm a horrible person," or "Even though I killed those people."

And as they rub this spot, we're going to have them repeat that three times: "Even though I can't sleep at night, I deeply and completely accept myself."

Affirmations remind a lot of people of Stuart Smalley, the affirmation guy from Saturday Night Live. His affirmation was, "I'm good enough, I'm smart enough, and doggone it, people like me." It's interesting when that parody of therapy and self-help came out, a lot of people got a pretty good chuckle from it. But it's really a great affirmation: "I'm good enough, I'm smart enough, and doggone it, people like me."

Ever since then, we've been actually teaching clients, "Hey, use that affirmation from Stuart Smalley." They get a chuckle out of it.

Affirmations work for two reasons:

1. Literally, an affirmation replaces the constant self-defeating mantras that subconsciously we are repeating to ourselves all day long.
2. It challenges cognitive errors.

EFT affirmations are structured as they are in order to pace and lead; the "even though" part paces the current situation while the "I deeply and completely accept myself" leads the clients to where they need to be. The client might believe the part that says, "even though I can't sleep at night" or "even though I keep seeing a picture of the bull goring me" or "even though everyone thinks I'm crazy" or "even though my wife is going to leave me." The client might not believe the second part—the part about self-love and self-acceptance—when they're saying the affirmation.

But when your client says the affirmation, especially three times, then it forces them to question: "I wonder if that's true. I wonder if I could." This is all a subconscious process. "I wonder if I could love myself and accept myself deeply." In order to create "I wonder if," your clients have to visualize and experience themselves loving themselves and caring for themselves. That actually tricks them into creating that state of self-love and self-caring.

It really becomes an experiential process of self-confrontation in cognitive behavioral therapy. It's no different than confrontation in CBT, but instead of sitting across the room and ending up in a power struggle where you confront your client, you get the client to self-challenge. You don't have get them in the now Fritz-Perls-style, break them through to the other side, or convince them to take the first step in a twelve-step program. The affirmation does that work for you.

With these techniques, we align with the client. This is a great tool to increase rapport. One of our processes in strategic intervention is Socratic dialogue, or metamodeling as they call it in neurolinguistic programming. Basically it's a matter of asking, "How do you know?"

> **Client:** "Everything is horrible, and my wife is going to leave me."

> **Therapist:** "Well, how do you know your wife is going to leave you? Is it possible she's not?"

But in this, we're not denying that. If they say, "My father didn't love me," we're not trying to reframe that. We're not challenging a cognitive error. We don't enter into a conflict-based, adversarial relationship with the client.

We simply take them as they present themselves: "All right, your father didn't love you." In EFT, you rub a spot and repeat, "Even though my father didn't love me, I deeply and completely accept myself."

There's a point called the karate chop point. The reason they call it that is it's the meaty part of the outside of the palm or the inside of the palm, if you were a karate student. Alternatively, you can tap that and say, "Even though I have this pain," or "Even though I can't sleep at night, I deeply and completely accept myself." Repeat three times.

We always tap along with clients. That's another way of being in rapport with them. You're modeling for them. If you don't do that, your client might become self-conscious being silly. But if we're silly together, now this is normal.

We're going to tap each point in the sequence six to eight times. That six to eight times is simply going to be the number of times that you tap as you're repeating the affirmation three times. It should be natural. You probably won't even need to count it.

It doesn't matter if you tap with two fingers or three. Dave normally taps with two fingers and has his clients tap with two fingers. It's what's natural for him now. It's Dave's ritual.

There are seven different points used in EFT. As we go through them, try this out yourself. You can use whatever issue or concern you with to address. When we do what we ask our clients to do, it actually makes us better therapists.

The eyebrow point is right on the ridge of the eyebrow. It's basically on the top of the orbit and right where the eyebrow ends by your nose. Tap that and repeat the affirmation.

We'll use procrastination as an example:

> *"Even though I procrastinate, I deeply and completely accept myself."*

The second point is called the side of the eye. It's on the orbit again. It's on the opposite end of the eyebrow. You'll see a lot of people tapping their temple, but that's actually not the point. It's on the orbital of the eye. It's on the ridge.

However, based on Harper's theory, any stimulation of the upper part of the body produces the same result, even if you missed the "energy meridian" point.

Dave tends to favor the idea that the ritual is the change rather than the premise that Chinese medicine is the answer. Even so, he tends to demonstrate the traditional points in case the client goes home and gets on YouTube and looks at it and says, "That's a different point than I'm tapping." That can create a little bit of dissonance in them and affects their belief.

We act on whatever we believe. If your clients believe, "I was taught by my therapist correctly," then they will act in a way that increases success. But if your clients think, "My therapist taught me incorrectly," they will believe that this isn't going to work for them, and they might even find themselves worse off. Or they might just think, "I'm even more confused than I was."

So the next point is on the orbital and again we repeat, "Even though I procrastinate, I deeply and completely accept myself. Even though I procrastinate, I deeply and completely accept myself. Even though I procrastinate, I deeply and completely accept myself."

The next point is the under the eye point. It's still along the orbital on the ridge underneath the eye. Tap and repeat three times: "Even though I procrastinate, I deeply and completely accept myself. Even though I procrastinate, I deeply and completely accept myself. Even though I procrastinate, I deeply and completely accept myself."

Then under the nose: just the midpoint between the lip and the nose. "Even though I procrastinate, I deeply and completely accept myself. Even though I procrastinate, I deeply and completely accept myself. Even though I procrastinate, I deeply and completely accept myself." It works, even if you have a moustache.

The next point is the chin point. It's between the lip and the chin, kind of in the divot. "Even though I procrastinate, I deeply and completely accept myself. Even though I procrastinate, I deeply and completely accept myself. Even though I procrastinate, I deeply and completely accept myself."

With the PTSD client, you may be dealing with, "Even though I have these images, I deeply and completely accept myself. Even though I have these images, I deeply and completely accept myself. Even though I have these images, I deeply and completely accept myself."

Or "Even though the accident was my fault, I deeply and completely accept myself."

Whatever belief they're giving you, you can use with EFT. It can build around a cognitive process. It can be around visions. It can be around a physical sensation. It can be around a belief. Any of those things that the DSM-5 pointed out as stressors in the PTSD client's experience can be the basis of an EFT session.

The next point is the collarbone point. That's right where the collarbone meets with the breastbone. It's the point that's the most prominent point. There should be a nice resounding thud when people tap that. Again, "Even though I procrastinate, I deeply and completely accept myself. Even though I procrastinate, I deeply and completely accept myself. Even though I procrastinate, I deeply and completely accept myself."

The next point is under the arm. For men, it will be sort of nipple line kind of medial underneath the armpit. For women, typically it's along the bra line. You just tap that as you repeat your mantra three times. "Even though I procrastinate, I deeply and completely accept myself. Even though I procrastinate, I deeply and completely accept myself. Even though I procrastinate, I deeply and completely accept myself."

We'll go to the hands. Some people include the hands. Some people don't.

We're going to go ahead and teach it to you simply so you'll have the entire recipe. You may find for whatever reason that people get an emotional charge at certain points, so you may stay on that point longer.

Somebody may say, "I just can't sleep at night. I see these really bad images when I close my eyes to lie down. I can't get comfortable and I toss and turn."

You could do, "Even though I can't sleep at night," and then you could go back over it with, "Even though I toss and turn at night," and then you could go back over it, "Even though I see these vivid…"

One of the reasons we collected all of the sensory data in the very beginning is we can use every single one of those. We can go through this several times using all the different elements of it.

If they're saying, "I eat five Snickers a day," we could ask, "Well, what do you like about Snickers?"

"Oh, it's just so crunchy and sugary. It feels so good when it's melting in my mouth."

So the affirmation could be, "Even though it feels so good when it's melting in my mouth." You can go through the whole gamut.

Really understand your client's model of their experience with this, their subjective experience, and you can tap on all those.

Then we're going to go on the top of the fingers. It's going to be above the first knuckle, near the fingertip. When I say the top of each finger, what I mean is if you were to hold your hand out with your thumb up, that's the top.

First we're going to tap on the top of the thumb. We're going to repeat the mantra "Even though I procrastinate, I deeply and completely accept myself. Even though I procrastinate, I deeply and completely accept myself. Even though I procrastinate, I deeply and completely accept myself."

Next finger: "Even though I procrastinate, I deeply and completely accept myself. Even though I procrastinate, I deeply and completely accept myself. Even though I procrastinate, I deeply and completely accept myself."

The middle finger: "Even though I procrastinate, I deeply and completely accept myself. Even though I procrastinate, I deeply and completely accept myself. Even though I procrastinate, I deeply and completely accept myself."

We're going to skip the ring finger and go straight to the pinky: "Even though I procrastinate, I deeply and completely accept myself. Even though I procrastinate, I deeply and completely accept myself. Even though I procrastinate, I deeply and completely accept myself."

Then we can do the karate chop: "Even though I procrastinate, I deeply and completely accept myself. Even though I procrastinate, I deeply and completely accept myself. Even though I procrastinate, I deeply and completely accept myself. Even though I procrastinate, I deeply and completely accept myself."

Now there's also a process when you're done with that called the nine-gamut. A lot of EFT practitioners have actually dropped the nine-gamut from their EFT recipe. We're going to show it to you anyway, but just know that you could probably go through this process a couple times and test to see if you think that the nine-gamut is needed.

The reason we skipped the ring finger earlier is the nine gamut starts by tapping the area between the pinky and the ring finger and about a half inch up from the knuckles. We're going to tap that, and as we're tapping it, we're going to close our eyes, we're going to open our eyes, we're going to look down hard right without moving the head, come back to center, look down hard left. Again, you may see some EMDR similarities here. Look down hard left without moving your head.

Then you're going to roll your eyes in a clockwise direction, roll your eyes in a counter-clockwise direction. Then you're going to hum two seconds of any song whether it's *Mary Had a Little Lamb* or *Row, Row, Row Your Boat*, and then count quickly from one to five (1, 2, 3, 4, 5) and then hum again. That's it.

Even though that's simple, you will probably have to practice it a couple of times to get it committed to memory. If you are working with a client, you will want to practice with them at the beginning, middle, and end of the session and give them a recording or send them to YouTube so they can actually practice it. You want it to become a habit they can engage in.

One of the other aspects of this is, especially once you start humming *Row, Row, Row Your Boat* is it's simply a distraction technique. It's about thinking about something else. If you spend all your time thinking about your trauma and you don't practice thinking about something else, it will become normal for you to be traumatized. It won't be normal for you to think about something else. Thus, it's a great pattern interrupt.

The Buddhist writer Thich Nhat Hanh talks about being grateful for his non-toothache. He says, "My tooth does not hurt today. I am grateful for my non-toothache."

The point is we often are only aware of our teeth when we have a toothache. When our teeth are fine, we're not aware of our non-toothache, even though we have a lot more non-toothaches than toothaches.

It's like our feet. You really only notice your feet when you start to develop a blister. You walk all day long and you don't at all think about your feet typically unless your shoes are too tight or you develop a blister. Suddenly you notice every single step you take.

At your own leisure, take ten minutes and go through this EFT process yourself, dealing with your own issue. Practice this several times over the next couple of days before you ever apply this with a client. Test it yourself and find out if it's a useful tool for you. If it's a useful tool for you, you'll be able to pass that useful tool on to others with passion.

Once we've done the entire process, we're going to check once again their Subjective Units of Distress and see if there's been any change. You can actually speed up this process after doing it the first time. You could say, "This procrastination, this procrastination, this procrastination, this procrastination, this procrastination, this procrastination." That quickly you could take them through it over and over again. You can focus on a certain point. "This procrastination, this procrastination."

We're going to do that until we get some resolution. We don't need to get to zero.

If they come in and they're stressed at a level nine, they may be willing to try this without you having to convince them because they'll do anything no matter how silly it is. If you can get them to a six, they'll do it again. A six is great.

We really don't celebrate partial success enough in therapy. We want full resolution of a symptom. But if we can get them from a nine to a six, that's cause to celebrate. Any decrease in symptoms, any improvement in a condition, is a victory.

Sometimes a thirty percent change is the difference between going to jail and remaining free. Perhaps at a nine, your client exercises poor impulse control and desperate coping strategies. But at a six, your client might use a coping strategy that—while it may not be the most helpful thing in the world—is not the one that will land them in jail.

The other thing we have to realize is if we have a client who has been living, for instance, with post-traumatic stress disorder for a year or two or ten, they may not be quite ready to let all of it go yet because they have no idea what their life will look like afterwards. It's become a source of certainty for them. There may be serious secondary gain in having it.

If they're veterans, they're getting disability, money, and education. We're not saying that this is why they're doing it. They're not experiencing PTSD so they can get benefits, but once they get the benefits, there's an incentive to stay sick. It is almost a catch-22. You're no longer eligible for the benefits you couldn't afford yourself. From a financial perspective, it's true.

It's also true even in a relationship perspective. In the case of a disabled PTSD survivor, maybe his wife has been caring enough about him to take the responsibility of working and caring for the family. Now if he gets well, that means he's going to have to give up building ships out of matchboxes in the garage because he has to go to work eight hours a day. It's not that he really minds working eight hours a day as a Wal-Mart greeter, but he really prefers building ships out of matchboxes.

And if he hasn't been to work in three years, it's kind of frightening to go back to that, especially if he's in a field like med-tech, paramedic, police officer, or even in a field like a graphic designer. Once he is actually doing well enough to consider going back into the workforce, he may find that the change in technology in the graphic arts business has changed to an overwhelming, frustrating, and even scary degree.

When dealing with this, we have to look at resiliency and transition issues. Just like in the military, when a soldier is coming home, you have to look at the transition issues they may be facing because it may not be beneficial for them to give up post-traumatic stress disorder in their model of the world.

EFT Storytelling Method

The next method we're going to talk about with EFT and PTSD is the storytelling method. This method is great when a person has a story that's running over and over and over in their minds. If a person ran a red light and hit a car, if a person was in combat, you're actually going to have them tell the story of the event.

Typically in hypnosis and things like that, we really don't want to do regression for trauma. We don't want to revivify the experience. In this case, though, we are revivifying because we're looking basically for the heads of wheat. We're going to cut those off as we go.

As they tell their story, your instructions for them are going to be, "I want you to start telling me the story and as soon as you start feeling anxious I want you to let me know."

Client: We went out on a combat patrol. We were driving down the road and I saw an Afghani running off. I'm starting to feel anxious now. I started to get worried there.

[We're going to find the SUDs on each one of those.]

Therapist: So when you saw that Afghani running off, as you're thinking about it now, where are you? As you see that Afghani running off in your memory, where's your level?

[We're going to work each one of those issues independently.]

Client: I'm a six. Now I'm a two.

Therapist: So what happens next? Continue the story.

Client: Then we're driving and I hear a large boom.

Therapist: And as you hear that large boom, what's your level of anxiety?

Client: It's at an eight right now.

[Or it might go like this:]

Client: I saw the Humvee in front of me explode.

Therapist: What's your level of anxiety?

Client: It's an eight.

Therapist: So tap "Even though the Humvee in front of me...."

[Or you may need to ask for details:]

Therapist: What did you think when you saw the Humvee explode?

Client: Well, my best friend, Bob, was in that Humvee, and I thought of his wife and his family.

> **Therapist:** So tap "Even though my best friend Bob may
> be dead..." or "Even though his wife and his family
> may lose Bob..."

Whatever comes up, we're going to tap on that.

We're going to go through the entire story and tap on every single incident in that story that causes distress and anxiety.

Working Content-Free

If a veteran does not want to talk to you, if your client doesn't want to tell you the story, if you don't have that level of trust, you can do this content-free. You can have them think through the story or what's bothering them in their own mind and simply say when they feel anxious.

They can go through in their own mind the part of the story that's distressing: "See yourself in that situation. You don't have to tell me what it is, but when you get to a point where you feel anxious, let me know."

They say, "Okay, I feel anxious now."

Then you coach them: "Even though I feel anxious now..." or "Even though I'm remembering this now..." or "Even though this event happened..." or whatever it is that they're doing. They can say, "Even though I feel anxious right now, I deeply and completely accept myself."

Some therapists take it personally when a client won't share the details of their trauma. In truth, you don't need to know the details of their trauma because it's really not relevant to your ability to create an intervention to help them. You want to be able to guide them through this process without becoming lost in the details of that experience. There's a danger when the client verbalizes that the therapist will decide what the therapist thinks is important and then project that perception onto the client, rather than simply letting the client understand what's important.

A lot of times when we're working with clients, we may get sucked into the content, when really what we need to do most of the time is focus on the structure of their subjective reality and what's happening—not necessarily what the specifics of their subjective reality are.

That's one reason EFT can be an effective intervention for a client who has taken the life of another, especially if that client has PTSD.

AFTERWORD: RETURN TO OZ

The little girl grew angry when she saw she had lost one of her pretty shoes and said to the witch, "Give me back my shoe!"

"I won't!" retorted the witch, laughing, "for it is now my shoe, not yours, and someday I shall get the other one from you, too."

This made Dorothy so very angry. She picked up a bucket of water and dashed it over the witch, wetting her from head to foot. The wicked creature shrieked, and then she began to shrink. "See what you've done!" she screamed. "I'm going to melt away!"

"I'm very sorry, indeed," said Dorothy, who was truly frightened to see the witch actively melting before her very eyes.

"I never thought a little girl like you would ever be able to melt me and my wicked deeds. Look out! Here I go!"

And with these words, the witch fell down into a melted, shapeless mass and began to spread over the kitchen floor.

— An excerpt from "The Wizard of Oz" by L. Frank Baum

It's odd to think about the sweet little girl from Kansas having a body count of two—one accidental death and the other a (possibly intentional) homicide—but as we've seen, there's no such thing as a killer; there are simply people who have killed. These are unique individuals with unique reactions and unique needs.

Yet there is something all of them need: individualized help, acceptance, and support from someone like you.

KEYNOTE SPEAKING, CONFERENCE TRAINING, AND IN-HOUSE TRAINING FOR PROFESSIONAL GROUPS

Dr. Richard K. Nongard and David Parke, are available together or separately to provide valuable training on this subject or other topics related to leadership, counseling and helping other people.

Bring Dr. Richard K. Nongard and/or David Parke to your professional group.

Contact Information:

Dr. Richard K. Nongard

Peachtree Professional Education, Inc.

15560 N. Frank L. Wright Blvd. B4-118 Scottsdale, AZ 85260

(918) 236-6116 or (702) 488-9640

richard@fastceus.com or visit www.RichardNongard.com